American Catholics

American Catholics

Edited by

Joseph F. Kelly

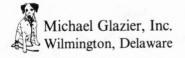

Michael Glazier, Inc.
Wilmington, Delaware

First published in 1989 by Michael Glazier, Inc., 1935 West Fourth Street, Wilmington, Delaware 19805.

Library of Congress Cataloging-in-Publication Data

Catholicism : the American experience
    p. cm. —
    ISBN 0-89453-775-X
    1. Catholic Church—United States—History. 2. United States—Church history. I. McBrien, Richard P. II. Series.
BX1406.2.C38 1989
282' .73—dc20
                                             89-7638
                                                CIP

Cover Design by Pat Harris
Typography by Phyllis Boyd LeVane
Printed in the United States of America

TABLE OF CONTENTS

Catholicism:
The American Experience

Richard P. McBrien
University of Notre Dame

I should insist at the outset that by "American" I mean that which pertains to the United States of America. Just as Catholics have learned not to equate "Church" with "Catholic Church" as if there were only one Church, so Americans are learning not to equate America with the United States as if all of South America and the rest of North America were somehow less "American."

I write neither as an historian nor as a sociologist, but as a theologian. More specifically, as an ecclesiologist. In treating the topic, therefore, I have no intention of trying to improve upon the work of American church historians like John Tracy Ellis, Martin Marty, James Hennesey, Jay Dolan, Gerald Fogarty, Philip Gleason, and David O'Brien, nor upon the work of sociologists like Robert Bellah, John Coleman, Philip Murnion, and Andrew Greeley. There are many important things to say about the American Catholic experience that I shall not be saying, either because I lack space for it or, what is more likely, the professional competence.[1]

---

[1]See also my essay, "The American Contribution to Ecclesiology," in *The Catholic Church: The United States Experience*, Irene Woodward, ed., (New York: Paulist

My purpose, therefore, is limited. I shall ask, and seek to answer the following questions:

(1) Has the American experience directly or indirectly shaped American Catholicism's self-understanding as a church? If so, how?

(2) To what extent, if any, is there a fundamental congruence between the American political tradition and Catholicism?

(3) Has Catholicism, in its own turn, directly or indirectly shaped the American experience itself? If so, how?

(4) Are recent developments in Catholic theology and practice more, or less, congruent with the American political tradition?

(5) What effect are these developments likely to have on the American Catholic experience of the future?

I. The Influence of America on Catholicism

Has the American experience directly or indirectly shaped American Catholicism's self-understanding as a church? If so, how?

I should suggest that the American experience has, at most, *indirectly* influenced American Catholicism's self-understanding as a church. Furthermore, that influence has been of a very mixed kind. In some instances, the American experience has served merely to reinforce already existing elements of the Catholic tradition. These elements include constitutionalism (which, as Brian Tierney reminds us, the Church itself was largely responsible for initiating in the Western world[2]), par-

---

Press, 1979), pp. 73-89; my article, "Catholicism: *E Pluribus Unum*," in *Daedalus* 111 (winter 1982) 73-83 (reprinted in *Religion and America: Spirituality in a Secular Age*, Mary Douglas and Stephen M. Tipton, eds. [Boston: Beacon Press, 1983]), pp. 179-89); and my *The Remaking of the Church: An Agenda for Reform* (New York: Harper & Row, 1973), especially chapter 3, pp. 71-136.

[2]See Brian Tierney, "Roots of Western Constitutionalism in the Church's Own Tradition: the Significance of the Council of Constance," in *We, the People of God*

ticipation in the selection of leaders,[3] and due process of law.[4] Each of these topics has to do with the way the Church operates internally, and each has been the subject of important interdisciplinary studies sponsored by the Canon Law Society of America. I should argue, in fact, that the leading role played by the American Catholic Church in ecclesiastical renewal and reform has not been unrelated to America's own experience of, and historic commitment to, constitutional government and democracy.

In some other instances, the American experience (apart from its commitment to constitutionalism and democracy) has had a deleterious effect on Catholic self-understanding and mission. The American penchant for activism and pragmatism has, until recently, undermined American Catholicism's commitment to the intellectual life, a problem dramatically highlighted by Msgr. John Tracy Ellis' famous address on May 14, 1955, before the Catholic Commission on Intellectual and Cultural Affairs at Maryville College, in St. Louis,[5] and further examined by sociologist Thomas O'Dea[6] and theologian Gustave Weigel, S.J.[7] This indifference, if not hostility, to the intellectual life has denied the American Catholic Church a

... *a Study of Constitutional Government for the Church,* James A. Coriden, ed. (Huntington, IN: Our Sunday Visitor Press, 1968), pp. 113-28.

[3]See *The Choosing of Bishops: Historical and Theological Studies,* William Bassett, ed. (Hartford, CT: Canon Law Society of America, 1971), and *Who Decides for the Church? Studies in Co-Responsibility,* James Coriden, ed. (Hartford, CT: Canon Law Society of America, 1971).

[4]See *The Case for Freedom: Human Rights in the Church,* James Coriden, ed. (Washington: Corpus Books, 1969), and *On Due Process: A Summary of Actions Taken by the National Conference of Catholic Bishops on the Subject of Due Process* (Washington: United States Catholic Conference, 1970). See also Nelson J. Callahan, *A Case for Due Process in the Church* (Staten Island, NY: Alba House, 1970).

[5]See "American Catholics and the Intellectual Life," *Thought* 30 (1955), pp. 351-88.

[6]*American Catholic Dilemma: An Inquiry into Intellectual Life* (New York: Sheed & Ward, 1958).

[7]"*American Catholic Intellectualism*—a Theologian's Reflections," *Review of Politics* 19 (1957), pp. 275-307.

learned clergy through most of its history. This may explain, to some extent at least, the failure of the American bishops to exercise any significant leadership at the Second Vatican Council (apart from their intervention in the debate on religious liberty), and the tendency of priests over the years to fall victim too easily to the seducements of doctrinal and biblical fundamentalism on the one hand, and to theologically superficial piety on the other. We have been more comfortable discussing the "Hail Mary pass" than the intricacies of Mariology. Indeed, we have settled for the worst sort of Marian piety, while demanding the very best from the football team at the university named in her honor.

Individualism is another characteristic of the American experience. Although Catholicism is a strongly social and communal tradition, the impact of individualism is more pronounced now than before, as Robert Bellah's recent study suggests.[8] Individualism is especially apparent in the upwardly-mobile Catholic population, where the "free to choose" mentality, encapsulated in economist Milton Friedman's book of the same title, has taken hold. Recent voting behavior indicates that American Catholics are less sensitive than ever before in their history to the interests of the poor and the socially marginal. Their obvious lack of enthusiasm for the U.S. Catholic bishops' pastoral letter on the economy is a case-in-point.

American Catholics, in increasingly large numbers, are rejecting, or at least choosing to ignore, some of the principal tenets of Catholic social doctrine. The American experience, as it has evolved and expressed itself in the politics of the 1980s, seems to be enticing many Catholics away from their own tradition and closer to Pelagianism ("God helps those who help themselves") and an extreme Calvinism ("Prosperity is a sign of God's favor; poverty is a sign of God's displeasure").

Our bishops have their work cut out for them.

[8]Robert Bellah, *et al.*, *Habits of the Heart: Individualism and Commitment in American Life* (Berkeley: University of California Press, 1985).

II. Catholicism and the American Political Tradition

To what extent, if any, is there a fundamental congruence between the American political tradition and Catholicism?

For Alexis de Tocqueville, the French social philosopher, one of the most fascinating characteristics of 19th century America was the comfortable manner in which Catholics seemed to be getting on in the new world. He noted that the original English settlers had been people who had "shaken off the pope's authority [and] acknowledged no other religious supremacy."[9] They brought to America a Christianity which de Tocqueville could only describe as democratic and republican. America should have been as politically foreign to Catholics as it was denominationally and geographically.

Fifty years earlier (de Tocqueville published the 12th edition of his *Democracy in America* in 1848, so he is referring here to the turn of the century) Ireland had begun pouring a Catholic population into the United States. At the same time, American Catholics were making converts. By the middle of the 19th century there were more than a million Catholics in the United States.

De Tocqueville observed these Catholics to be "very loyal in the practice of their worship and full of zeal and ardor for their beliefs. Nevertheless," he continued with some amazement, "they form the most republican and democratic of all classes in the United States. At first glance this is astonishing, but reflection easily indicates the hidden causes thereof."[10]

He directly challenged the assumption that Catholicism is the natural enemy of democracy. "Rather," he continued, "among the various Christian doctrines Catholicism seems one of those most favorable to equality of conditions."

[9]*Democracy in America*, George Lawrence, trans. (Garden City, NY: Doubleday/Anchor, 1969), p. 288.

[10]*Idem.*

Tocqueville's reasoning, however, was original, to say the least. "For Catholics," he wrote, "religious society is composed of two elements: priest and people. The priest is raised above the faithful; all below him are equal."

"In matters of dogma the Catholic faith places all intellects on the same level; the learned man and the ignorant, the genius and the common herd, must all subscribe to the same details of belief; rich and poor must follow the same observances, and it imposes the same austerities upon the strong and the weak; it makes no compromise with any mortal, but applying the same standard to every human being, it mingles all classes of society at the foot of the same altar, just as they are mingled in the sight of God."

"Catholicism," he continued, "may dispose the faithful to obedience, but it does not prepare them for inequality. However, I would say that Protestantism in general orients men much less toward equality than toward independence."

"Catholicism is like an absolute monarchy. The prince apart, conditions are more equal there than in republics."

" ... (N)o men are more led by their beliefs than are Catholics to carry the idea of equality of conditions over into the political sphere."[11]

De Tocqueville attributed some of this democratic fervor to the economic and demographic status of the Catholic population. Most Catholics were poor and in the minority. For these two reasons they may have been led, "perhaps in spite of themselves," as de Tocqueville put it, "toward political doctrines which, maybe, they would adopt with less zeal were they rich and predominant." (Recent Catholic voting behavior seems to bear him out.)

The Catholic clergy, he noted, seemed to have supported this arrangement. They carefully divided the world into two realms: the realm of revealed dogmas to which Catholics must

[11]*Ibid.*, pp. 288-9.

submit themselves without discussion, and the realm of political truth which, according to the priests, God had left to our free investigation. "Thus," de Tocqueville concluded, "American Catholics are both the most obedient of the faithful and the most independent citizens."[12]

What the French Catholic layman, Alexis de Tocqueville, had observed in the mid-19th century, the American Jesuit theologian, John Courtney Murray, verified in the mid-20th century. In his modern classic, *We Hold These Truths: Catholic Reflections on the American Proposition*, Murray argued that the American consensus was entirely consistent with the Catholic tradition.

"Historically," he wrote, "this tradition has found, and still finds, its intellectual home within the Catholic Church. It is indeed one of the ironies of history that the tradition should have so largely languished in the so-called Catholic nations of Europe at the same time that its enduring vigor was launching a new Republic across the broad ocean. There is also some paradox," Murray continued, "in the fact that a nation which has (rightly or wrongly) thought of its own genius in Protestant terms should have owed its origins and the stability of its political structure to a tradition whose genius is alien to current intellectualized versions of the Protestant religion, and even to certain individualistic exigencies of Protestant religiosity.... The point here is that Catholic participation in the American consensus—the ethical and political principles drawn from the tradition of natural law—approve themselves to the Catholic intelligence and conscience. Where this kind of language is talked, the Catholic joins the conversation with complete ease. It is his language. The ideas expressed are native to his own universe of discourse. Even the accent, being American, suits his tongue."[13]

[12]*Ibid.*, p. 289.

[13]P. 41. Avery Dulles, however, is more cautious about affirming a congruence between Catholicism and the American political tradition. He thinks this passage

This is not to say, of course, that there weren't some rocky parts of the road in between de Tocqueville and Murray. The so-called Americanism controversy disclosed a tension—then as now perhaps—between the distinctively American Catholic experience and that of Catholics outside America, particularly in Rome.

The English-speaking, largely Irish, Catholic majority generally sided with those Protestants who saw America as, to use the words of Martin Marty, "a phoenix grave of European nationalities."[14] While religious differences would remain, ethnic boundaries would mean progressively less until a fused Catholic people emerged. The German immigrants defended an opposing model. They feared Irish domination and fought to maintain their own ethnic boundaries, with their languages, customs, and ecclesiastical independence.

In Cincinnati, for example, one German priest feared that his people might drift toward the American way, with its "hotbed of fanaticism, intolerance and radical ultra views on matters of politics and religion." His people must stay German to fight off the American nationality, which bred "all the vagaries of spiritualism, Mormonism, free-loveism, prohibition, infidelity, and materialism."[15]

Though himself a man of Irish provincial mentality, Cardinal James Gibbons of Baltimore had a grand vision of a united American Catholic Church. So committed was he to the elimination of factionalism within the Church that he even wrote a letter sympathizing with the complaints against the Irish by Father Peter Abbelen, the representative of the

---

somewhat exaggerated. See his "Vatican II and the American Experience of Church," in *Vatican II: Open Questions and New Horizons*, Gerald M. Fagin, ed. (Wilmington, DE: Michael Glazier, Inc., 1984) p. 42.

[14] *Pilgrims in Their Own Land: 500 Years of Religion in America* (Boston: Little, Brown and Company, 1984; New York: Penguin Books, 1985), p. 280.

[15] Cited by Marty, p. 281.

German-born archbishop of Milwaukee, Michael Heiss. Unfortunately, Father Abbelen flaunted the document in Rome. Some of Gibbons' friends in the American hierarchy, Keane and Ireland, wondered aloud how he could have given such a weapon to "this secret emissary of a clique of German Bishops among us." The letter was innocent enough, but there was enough in it to give plausibility to the argument that Gibbons and his allies were trying to Americanize Germans and thereby lead them away from the Church.

Gibbons explained to Rome that he refused absolutely to recognize any ethnic distinction in the government of the Church, and that such distinctions would give rise to a divisive spirit of nationalism. He also wrote one bishop that he wanted to ward off a "war of the races" that would only vindicate charges of enemies that American Catholicism was a "religion of foreigners."

Rome accepted Gibbons' report. But the conflict heated up again when Peter Paul Cahensly, a Rhineland merchant who arrived in 1883 to establish an organization to care for German Catholic emigrants, pressed the German theme, playing on fears that atheists, infidels, and Protestants would lure neglected Catholics from the faith.

Gibbons remained publicly calm, in spite of pressure from his episcopal allies to act severely against "the wicked wretch Cahensly." He tried to win over the German bishops in America in his war against an "Americo-European conspiracy" to take over various American dioceses. Gibbons preached a courageous sermon in Milwaukee in which he said, "Brothers we are, whatever may be our nationality.... Loyalty to God's Church and to our Country!"

At a Catholic congress connected with the 1893 world's fair in Chicago, the papal legate, Archbishop Francisco Satolli surprised many non-Catholics with his ringing endorsement of the U.S. Constitution. "Christian truth and American liberty," he said, "will make you free, happy and prosperous."

But the drama continued. Catholic participation in the

accompanying World's Parliament of Religions was marred by a garbled account of it by a Protestant journalist, who thought he heard Gibbons say that for him the attraction of Catholicism was its system of charities more than its faith and morals or its apostolic succession of bishops. The fires of controversy raged anew. Pope Leo XIII opened the new year of 1895 with his long-promised letter to the U.S. bishops, but it contained a sentence that "seemed to flush every leftover nativist out of the bushes," to use Martin Marty's words. It would be false, Pope Leo wrote, to hold up the American model of Church and State as the most desirable of all, given the way Church and State in America are "dissevered and divorced."

Some Europeans had invented a heresy, called it Americanism, and went out looking for people who might hold it. Conservative royalists in France seized on a translation of a *Life of Father Hecker* because it had a too-progressive preface which seemed to make Father Hecker more of a democrat than a Catholic. The royalists listed all its errors, and called them Americanism. Gibbons was furious. "I regard the attacks of Protestants as mild compared with the unprincipled course of these so-called Catholics." (Times haven't changed all that much.)

Pope Leo asked Satolli, who had by now gone completely over to the anti-Gibbons side, and Cardinal Camillo Mazzella to summarize the case against Americanism. On January 22, 1899, the Pope issued *Testem Benevolentiae*. Gibbons wrote the Pope that what the French called Americanism was absurd, extravagant, and unrepresented in America. From that point on, the air began seeping out of the balloon. People, inside and outside the Catholic Church, became increasingly indifferent to the whole issue.

By 1902 the controversy had ended. Pope Leo wrote Gibbons a very warm letter, praising the American Catholic Church for its "flourishing youthfulness" and assuring Gibbons that it brought delight to his heart. On June 29, 1908, Leo's successor, Pope Pius X, declared the United States no longer mission territory.

But the controversy had left scars. American Catholics generally had been unaffected by the encyclical, but Catholic intellectuals became more cautious. "Something of a deep freeze set in," James Hennesey writes, "deepened further in the new century by Roman condemnation of Modernism. American Catholics had known an inchoate moment of native constructive theological thought. They now slipped more or less peaceably into a half-century's theological hibernation."[16]

The issue, however, resurfaced in the pages of theological journals in the decades just prior to the Second Vatican Council. In 1945 Archbishop Edward Mooney of Detroit encouraged John Courtney Murray to interest himself in the problem of Church and State, which "had bedevilled the Catholic community in the United States since the time of John Carroll and had been at the root of so much division between Catholics and other Americans."[17] Murray accepted the suggestion and entered the discussion in the pages of the prestigious Jesuit quarterly, *Theological Studies*, which Murray edited. The opposing view was taken by Msgr. Joseph Clifford Fenton, professor at The Catholic University of America, in the pages of the journal *he* edited, the now-defunct *American Ecclesiastical Review*. Fenton was joined by Redemptorist Father Francis J. Connell, with important support also from Cardinal Alfredo Ottaviani, Prefect of the Supreme Congregation of the Holy Office. Fenton and Connell argued that the ideal state is one in which the Catholic Church is the established religion. Catholics accepted the American arrangement, they conceded, only as an expediency. If, however, demographic circumstances should ever change, the Catholic majority would be morally bound to work for a Catholic state

[16]*American Catholics: A History of the Roman Catholic Community in the United States* (New York: Oxford University Press, 1981), p. 203.

[17]*Ibid.*, p. 302.

and, at the same time, suppress all other forms of "false worship."

Murray went through some difficult times over this issue. In 1954 he was required to submit all of his writings to Rome for prior censorship, and for several years he published nothing on church-state relations. He was ignored during preparations for Vatican II and was not invited to its first session in 1962. To add insult to injury, in March 1963 he and three other Catholic theologians were banned by the rector, at the urging of the Apostolic Delegate, Archbishop Egidio Vagnozzi, from lecturing at The Catholic University of America. That same April, however, Cardinal Spellman, who did not particularly like Vagnozzi, had Pope John XXIII name Murray a *peritus* for the second session and thereafter. Finding on his arrival that the proposed conciliar document on religious liberty had been dropped from the agenda, Murray persuaded the American bishops, with Cardinal Spellman in the lead, to demand its restoration. (We'll come back to that document in due course.)

In the midst of all this, a Catholic layman named John Fitzgerald Kennedy was nominated by the Democratic Party as its standard-bearer in the 1960 presidential campaign. In his famous address before the Greater Houston Ministerial Association, candidate Kennedy said: "I believe in an America that is officially neither Catholic, Protestant, nor Jewish; where no public official either requests or accepts instructions on public policy from the pope, the National Council of Churches, or any other ecclesiastical source; where no religious body seeks to impose its will directly or indirectly upon the general populace or the public acts of its officials; and where religious liberty is so indivisible that an act against one church is treated as an act against all."

Alexis de Tocqueville would not have been surprised by John F. Kennedy. But his eyebrows might have arched in horror at the sight of so many of today's Catholics romping in bed with fundamentalist Protestants who bitterly opposed

Kennedy in 1960 simply because he was a Catholic, and whose forebears excoriated the papists from every platform.

III. *The Influence of Catholicism on America*

Has Catholicism, in its own turn, directly or indirectly shaped the American experience itself? If so, how?

My answer here is as brief as it is tentative. I should say that the influence has been mutual. Catholicism has been perhaps more influenced by the American experience than the American experience has been influenced by Catholicism. But this is a guess rather than a carefully grounded conclusion. Indeed, I don't know how such a conclusion could be established beyond reasonable doubt. I should prefer, therefore, to emphasize the mutuality of influence. If there is a congruence between Catholicism and the American political tradition, then whatever influence passes between them must travel along a two-way road. Whether there is more traffic heading in one direction than in another, I cannot say. In any case, it is a problem for historians, sociologists, and political scientists rather than for theologians. I should suspect that they would speak about Catholic influence exercised indirectly through the Democratic Party and in political life generally. It is only recently that the leadership of the Catholic Church has directly attempted to influence public policy debates in any serious and sophisticated way, but their first effort, the pastoral letter on nuclear war, seems to have got the bishops off to a reasonably good start.

Some might regard Catholicism's impact on America, especially in recent years, as more negative than positive. The abortion controversy, particularly as it affected the 1984 presidential election campaign, would normally be cited. But that issue doesn't admit of an easy analysis. First, if you're pro-choice, Catholic influence is a negative one. If you're anti-abortion but concerned about problems of law and consensus, as Governor Mario Cuomo is, the bishops' intervention assumes a different character, not entirely negative, but not entirely positive either. Finally, if you're simply trying to be faithful to the whole corpus of Catholic doctrine, you at least welcome the so-called "seamless garment" approach proposed by Cardinal Bernardin and generally endorsed by the National Conference of Catholic Bishops, with some highly visible exceptions.

In the final accounting, if we take seriously the arguments of Brian Tierney and John Courtney Murray that constitutionalism is, in fact, Catholicism's gift to the West, then, of course, the impact of Catholicism on the American political tradition is substantial.

IV. The Impact of Recent Catholic Developments on America

Are recent developments in Catholic theology and practice more, or less, congruent with the American political tradition?

Here I answer unhesitatingly. Recent developments in Catholic theology and life, especially those developments rooted in the Second Vatican Council, are entirely consistent with, and profoundly reinforce, the principal elements of the American political tradition.

The council's keynote document, *Lumen gentium*, the Dogmatic Constitution on the Church, changes the primary theological model of the Church from hierarchical institution to People of God. ("We, the People of God. . . .") The people are the Church. The mission belongs to all by baptism and confirmation, and not simply by hierarchical delegation. Every member of the Church must have access, in principle, to the process by which decisions which affect its life and mission are made. Authority is to be decentralized, without prejudice to the distinctive ministry of the Pope. The council even recommended specific instruments: national episcopal conferences, parish and diocesan councils, priests' senates, and the like.

(Shades of representative democracy, or, more precisely, of republicanism!) Pope Paul VI instituted regular international synods of bishops, and collegiality, although more honored perhaps in the breach than in the practice, became a new watchword and goal.

Nowhere, however, was the council's people-of-God ecclesiology more fully and more visibly manifested than in the liturgical renewal. Theory was brought dramatically into practice. The Eucharist was no longer the priest's business alone. It was the action of the whole worshipping assembly. All are called to participate in word, in gesture, and in song. Some are called to participate even more directly: as lectors, music directors, Eucharistic ministers, and so forth. The Eucharist is the highest form of participatory Catholicism. Alexis de Tocqueville would have been impressed and pleased.

A second major conciliar insight concerned the essentially pluralistic character of both Christianity and the human family itself. The Church is larger than the Catholic Church alone. It is composed of many churches which together constitute the one Church of Christ, albeit a divided Church. Furthermore, God works in many ways outside the Christian community, even through non-Christian religions. Pluralism requires respect for the rights of the many for the sake of the unity of the human family: *e pluribus unum*.

The council's teaching on this subject was essentially embodied in the document Father Murray helped to write, *Dignitatis humanae*, the Declaration on Religious Freedom.

Three doctrinal tenets are proposed therein: (1) an ethical doctrine stipulating that religious freedom is a human right (personal and collective); (2) a political doctrine specifying the functions and limits of government in matters religious; and (3) a theological doctrine supporting the freedom of the Church in the socio-political order. "A long-standing ambiguity" was finally clarified by the council, Murray wrote in a brief commentary on the document. "The Church does not deal with the secular order in terms of a double standard—freedom for the Church when Catholics are a minority, privilege for the Church and intolerance for others when Catholics are a majority."[18]

"The truth cannot impose itself except by virtue of its own truth," the council declared, "as it makes its entrance into the mind at once quietly and with power."[19] The council defined religious freedom as a matter of immunity "from coercion on the part of individuals or of social groups and of any human power, in such wise that in matters religious no one is to be forced to act in a manner contrary to his own beliefs. Nor is anyone to be restrained from acting in accordance with his own beliefs, whether privately or publicly, whether alone or in association with others, within due limits."[20]

The principle of religious freedom, so dear to the American political heart, is grounded in the "very dignity of the human person" and creates a right that must be "recognized in the constitutional law whereby society is governed. Thus it is to become a civil right."[21] It would "clearly transgress the limits set to its power" if the government were to "presume to direct or inhibit acts that are religious."[22]

Religious freedom is also grounded in the revealed word of God. "It is one of the major tenets of Catholic doctrine that man's response to God in faith must be free.... The act of faith is of its very nature a free act."[23]

We live in a world now, the council declared, in which nations are coming together into a closer unity and where people of different cultures and religions are being brought

[18] *The Documents of Vatican II*, Walter Abbot and Joseph Gallagher, eds. (New York: Guild, America, and Association Presses, 1966), p. 673.

[19] *Dignitatis humanae*, n. 1.

[20] *Ibid.*, n. 2.

[21] *Idem.*

[22] *Ibid.*, n. 3.

[23] *Ibid.*, n. 9.

together in closer relationships. "Consequently, in order that relationships of peace and harmony may be established and maintained within the whole of mankind, it is necessary that religious freedom be everywhere provided with an effective constitutional guarantee, and that respect be shown for the high duty and right of man to lead his religious life in society."[24]

Perhaps the most remarkable post-conciliar development which underscores the congruence of Catholicism and the American political tradition is the Code of Canon Law, specifically its so-called Bill of Rights (canons 208-31).

Canon 208 affirms, in words that would have brought utter delight to de Tocqueville's heart, that all the Christian faithful enjoy "a true equality with regard to dignity and the activity whereby all cooperate in the building up of the Body of Christ. . . ."

Other canons recognize the right of Church members to make their opinions known to pastors (c. 212 #3), and to establish associations for charitable and religious purposes and to hold meetings of such associations (c. 215). Those engaged in the sacred disciplines "enjoy a lawful freedom of inquiry and of prudently expressing their opinions on matters in which they have expertise" (c. 218). All Christians are to be "free from any kind of coercion in choosing a state in life" (c. 219). "No one is permitted to damage unlawfully the good reputation which another person enjoys nor to violate the right of another person to protect his or her own privacy" (c. 220). Catholics can defend their rights before a competent ecclesiastical court, and must always be judged by the norm of law (c. 221). "Lay Christians have the right to have recognized that freedom in the affairs of the earthly city which belongs to all citizens . . . " (c. 227). Lay persons also have the right to pursue a theological education (c. 229), and to exercise various ministries in the Church (c. 230), for which they have a right to "decent remu-

[24]*Ibid.*, n. 15.

neration," including pension, social security, and health benefits (c. 231).

In the old Code of Canon Law lay Catholics were essentially negative creatures. They were *not* clerics. They were *not* religious. They could *not* wear clerical or religious garb (c. 683, 1917 Code of Canon Law). The canonical leap, of course, could not have been made without the theological advances of this century and the official teachings of the Second Vatican Council. These developments, however, have solidified the positive relationship Catholics enjoy with the political traditions of "the new world."

V. The Future of Catholicism in America

What effect are these developments likely to have on the American Catholic experience of the future?

The participation of Catholics in the life of their Church and of their country will broaden and deepen. There is no turning back on the liturgical renewal, and nothing is more crucial to participatory Catholicism. All else will continue to depend on liturgical vitality: parish and diocesan councils, religious education, youth ministry, ministry to the sick, social ministries of various kinds, the stimulation of vocations to the ordained ministries and to the religious life, even involvement in the selection of pastoral leaders. The liturgy is the context in which the community assimilates, expresses, celebrates, and resolves to implement its fundamental understanding of itself and of its mission. It is no accident that traditionalist Catholics (and Archbishop LeFebvre is only the most extreme of them) should focus so sharply, and with so much anger, on the changes in the Mass. They see it for what it is, and for what the council said it is: "the summit toward which the activity of the Church is directed; at the same time it is the fountain from which all her power flows."[25] It is, therefore, "the primary and indispensable source from which the faithful are to derive the true Christian spirit."[26] To change the liturgy, therefore, is to do more than change rituals and rubrics. It is to change a way of being Church.

The Catholic Church, de Tocqueville wrote, "may dispose the faithful to obedience, but it does not prepare them for inequality." Rich and poor must follow the same observances, and the same austerities are imposed on the strong and the weak alike. And "it mingles all classes of society at the foot of the same altar, just as they are mingled in the sight of God."[27]

---

[25] *Sacrosanctum concilium*, Constitution on the Sacred Liturgy, n. 10.

[26] *Ibid.*, n. 14.

[27] *Op. cit.*, p. 288.

Religion in the Immigrant Community: 1820-1920

Jay P. Dolan
University of Notre Dame

Oscar Handlin began his prize-winning history, *The Uprooted*, with the statement: "Once I thought to write a history of the immigrants in America. Then I discovered that the immigrants were American history."[1]

Immigrants have been coming to this country ever since Columbus discovered the New World, almost 500 years ago. But the study of the United States as a nation of immigrants has been going on for not much more than 50 years. George Stephenson wrote what most consider the first scholarly history of immigration in 1924. Then in the 1930s the American-born son of Danish immigrants, Marcus Hansen, wrote a book, *The Atlantic Migration*, and this study marked the beginning of a sustained effort on the part of historians to write the history of immigration in the United States.[2]

An obvious question comes to mind—why did the historical study of immigration begin so late in our nation's history?

Throughout the nineteenth century when thousands upon

---

[1] Oscar Handlin, *The Uprooted* (Boston, 1951), p. 3.

[2] Marcus Hansen, *The Atlantic Migration 1607-1860* (Cambridge, Mass. 1940).

thousands of immigrants were arriving in the United States, historians were writing about the glories of colonial America and the revolutionary war. If people wrote about immigration, it was generally because they viewed it as a problem; a case in point would be Samuel F.B. Morse, noted painter and inventor. Morse wrote about the immigrants in the 1840s because he wanted to persuade people to keep them out of the country. The other most popular form of immigrant literature at this time was the pietistic, booster pamphlet or book that celebrated the glories of a particular immigrant group. Thomas D'Arcy McGee's book, *A History of the Irish Settlers in North America from the Earliest Period to the Census of 1850*, would be a good example of this type of literature.[3]

Once immigration came to a pause in the 1920s with the passage of new legislation, then for all practical purposes it ceased to be a problem; this allowed historians to analyze it in a more detached and unbiased manner. Nonetheless, the history of immigration remained outside the mainstream of American historical studies. Political history and the drama of soldiers at war continued to be the main focus of historians. For this reason relatively few people took up the challenge of Hansen, Oscar Handlin being the most noted of those that did.

What was true of American history in general was also true of the history of Christianity in particular. When Catholics wrote about their history, they wrote about bishops or the development of the institutional church. If they did write about immigration, their focus was most often on the issue of whether or not the immigrants kept the faith. When John Tracy Ellis wrote his short history of Catholicism in the late 1950s, he wrote that "one of the weakest areas in the literature on American Catholicism is immigration history. Aside from a

---

[3]Thomas D'Arcy McGee, *A History of the Irish Settlers in North America from the Earliest Period to the Census of 1850* (Boston, 1855).

few studies ... this rich field for research remains largely untilled."[4] When Protestants wrote the histories of their churches, they generally wrote about their leaders or about theological disputes. In other words, immigration history was as marginal to American church history as it was to American political and social history. This changed somewhat in the post-World War II era when scholars became interested in the question of what it meant to be an American. This issue of Americanization, of immigrants becoming American, sparked a new interest in immigration studies. As a result Catholic and Protestant church historians, Lutherans especially, began to reinterpret the past by making the phenomenon of Americanization their major interpretive concept.

As was true of much of American society, the 1960s ushered in a new era in historical studies. The social awakening of this decade made many people more conscious of their ethnic heritage and their identity as both immigrant and American. In the academy, historians were becoming more interested in social history, the history of the people and their culture, rather than just the history of Presidents and generals. These two developments sparked a renaissance in immigration history; coupled with this was the large increase in the number of college graduates as a result of the G.I. Bill and the subsequent increase in doctoral students in history. Immigration history suddenly was in and dissertations began to multiply like rabbits. The following statistic dramatically illustrates this development; of all the dissertations written on immigration between 1899 and 1972, 50 percent were done in one decade, 1962-72.[5] Reflecting this new development a group of American historians founded the Immigration History Society in 1965; shortly thereafter a newsletter began to be published to

[4]John Tracy Ellis, *American Catholicism* (Chicago, 1956), p. 195.

[5]Edward Kasinec, "Resources and Research Centers," in *Harvard Encyclopedia of American Ethnic Groups*, Steven Thernstrom, ed., (Cambridge, Mass. 1980), p. 876.

serve as a means of communication among immigration historians. On college campuses courses in immigration history became more commonplace. Centers for ethnic studies began to multiply and the publication of books related to immigration studies increased substantially. This new research changed the understanding of the American past and put the immigrants on the center stage of American history. In the 1960s and 70s people discovered what Oscar Handlin had realized in 1951, the immigrants were American history.[6]

Because of this renaissance in immigration studies we know a lot more about our immigrant ancestors. New theories about the immigrant experience have emerged and the place of religion in the lives of the people has been rediscovered and reevaluated.

One major intellectual development in immigration studies has been the reevaluation of the Americanization thesis. For much of the twentieth century historians accepted the theory that over the course of time, generally by the third generation, immigrants became Americanized. The metaphor most commonly used was that of the melting pot; though it could have a variety of meanings the melting pot generally conjured up the image of the immigrants being melted down so that they could become American. This thesis celebrated the unity of American culture and the assimilation of the immigrants to the American way of life.

The social awakening of the 1960s posed a mighty challenge to the Americanization thesis. There was a resurgence of ethnic or group consciousness both in America and abroad. The civil rights movement awakened Black Americans to a new and heightened self-consciousness; Hispanic Americans underwent a similar transformation. An ethnic revival took place among European immigrants and their descendants; buttons and

[6]Rudolph J. Vecoli, "The Resurgence of American Immigration History," *American Studies International* Vol. XVII, No. 2 (Winter 1979), pp. 46-66.

bumper stickers, parades and festivals celebrated the virtues of being ethnic. The implications of this for immigration studies were substantial. Not only did it foster an increased interest in immigration studies, but this ethnic renaissance led to a re-examination of the nation's past, most especially the Americanization thesis. As a result scholars began to champion the cultural pluralism of the nation, its diversity rather than its unity. Rather than stress the assimilation of immigrants to the American way of life, historians now emphasized how immigrant groups retained their Old World cultures. They stressed the retention of ethnic identity and the maintenance of cultural pluralism as important features of the American landscape. As a result of this, historians began to redirect their "research toward collecting evidence about the transmission of immigrant and ethnic identities from the Old World and about the retention or adaptation of cultural traits and social institutions in the New."[7] The popularity of social history reinforced this tendency by encouraging historians to do community studies of immigrant communities. What was previously looked upon as narrow, ethnocentric history became the vogue and more than one college professor was promoted to tenure because he or she had written a book on the Germans in Milwaukee or the Irish in New York.

A significant development that occurred simultaneously with the questioning of the Americanization thesis was the increased interest in Eastern and Southern European immigrants or those people historians call the new immigrants. Prior to the 1960s much of the historical study of immigrant groups focused on the old immigrants, the Irish and Germans. The ethnic renaissance of the 1960s changed this. Though they hardly neglected the old immigrants, historians now focused more

---

[7]Thomas J. Archdeacon, "Problems and Possibilities in the Study of American Immigration and Ethnic History," *International Migration Review*, Vol. 19, No. 1 (Spring 1985), p. 122.

attention on the immigrants from Eastern and Southern Europe. This obviously filled a need and scholars welcomed this development. But there was another aspect to this. By studying the new immigrants, Italians, Polish, Slovaks, Ukrainians and other Eastern European groups, historians were studying the most recently arrived European immigrants and quite naturally they would find evidence of the retention of old world cultures rather than evidence of pronounced assimilation and Americanization. Thus, the extensive research done in immigration studies in the last 20 years has tended to demonstrate that cultural pluralism rather than Americanization, diversity rather than unity, is the key to understanding the immigrant experience in the United States. It seems logical to expect that with the passage of time further study of the new immigrants will also reveal the validity of the assimilation or Americanization thesis. Another way of putting this is that the longer an immigrant group is present in the United States the more assimilated or Americanized they become.[8]

Who is correct, the Americanizers or the cultural pluralists? I suspect that this argument will go on for some time. Indicative of the diversity of opinion among scholars is the recent publication of two histories of immigration. One book takes the assimilationist, Americanizing position and thus the title— *Becoming American*; the other emphasizes the maintenance of old world cultures in America and is entitled—*TheTransplanted*. Both are fine studies but they approach the immigrant experience from two distinctly different points of view.[9]

How has this renaissance in immigration history affected religious history? In the last twenty-five years religious history has enjoyed its own revival and the trend toward social history,

[8]*Ibid.*, pp. 119-121.

[9]Thomas J. Archdeacon, *Becoming American: An Ethnic History* (New York, 1983) and John Bodnar, *The Transplanted*, (Bloomington, Indiana 1985).

so evident in other areas of the historical discipline, is also quite prominent in the field of American religious history. Moreover, historians of immigration are more aware of the importance of religion in the immigrant community and most often will incorporate this awareness into their study. A striking indication of this is that both of the most recent histories of immigration—*Becoming American* by Thomas Archdeacon and *The Transplanted* by John Bodnar—gives serious and substantial consideration to the religious dimension of the immigrant experience.

Such a development has considerably enhanced our understanding of the religious world of the immigrants. Unfortunately historians of American religion do not seem to be as in touch with the immigrant experience, either intellectually or experientially, and for that reason relatively few in-depth studies have been done of the religious world or the religious dimension of the immigrant experience. What this has meant is that our understanding of the religious world of the immigrants is not as developed as it should be, given the resurgence in immigration history in the last quarter century.[10]

While acknowledging this positive though limited state of affairs in the historical study of immigrant Christianity in the United States, we still know a lot more today about the role of religion in the immigrant community than we did twenty-five years ago.

In recent years historians have become intrigued with the big picture, the macro-view of history, and have put together diverse interpretive theories of history. One theory has to do with secularization; according to this interpretation the modern period of history proceeds along an increasingly secular course and with the passage of time religion becomes less important

---

[10]Indicative of this is, that of the 3,534 dissertations in immigration history written between 1885 and 1983 only 128 or 3.6 percent dealt with the topic of religion. I want to thank A. William Hoglund of the University of Connecticut who is putting together a bibliography of doctoral dissertations, 1885-1983, for this information.

and less meaningful. Another popular theory is the modernization thesis and in this interpretation religion likewise becomes a victim of enlightened ideas and progress. Applying this to the immigrant experience it is assumed that the religion of the old world would eventually disappear in the modern and secular setting of the new world.

The study of immigration history has demonstrated that this is not at all true. Indeed, the religion of the immigrants has changed over the course of time (the Jewish immigrant experience being the clearest example), but it has scarcely disappeared; in fact, religion not only persisted in the immigrant community but it acquired a new vigor and intensity. Precisely because of the experience of immigration, religion took on a dynamic quality and helped the immigrants in their adjustment to the New World. The historian, Timothy L. Smith, has argued this point very thoroughly and concluded that "migration and resettlement . . . altered the relationship between faith and ethnic identity by redefining the boundaries of peoplehood and by intensifying religious reflection and commitment."[11]

The first point that Smith made was that when the newcomers came to the United States "ethnic association . . . was determined largely by the immigrant's identification with a particular religious tradition." The clearest example of this would be the nineteenth century experience of German immigrants. Among the Germans were four distinct ethnic and religious communities: "a Protestant one, bounded by the Missouri and Wisconsin Lutheran Synods; a Jewish community . . . ; a small but influential community of freethinkers, united in the *Turnvereine*; and the German Catholics."[12] What Smith is suggesting is that religion outweighed the appeal of a common language, national feeling and belief in a common

---

[11]Timothy L. Smith, "Religion and Ethnicity in America," *American Historical Review*, Vol. 83, (December 1978), p. 1183.

[12]*Ibid.*, p. 1170.

descent as the chief organizing impulse in the immigrant community. How the immigrants went about this process of organization in defining their sense of peoplehood, or what can be called their ethnic identity, is very instructive. Again the Germans offer a good example of this process of community building or what Smith calls the "redefining" of "the boundaries of peoplehood."

The key institution in this organizing process among German Catholics was the parish. As one priest put it, the parish enabled them to "preserve incorrupt the sacred treasures of religion and to transmit it to their children."[13] In Philadelphia German Catholics organized their own parish as early as 1787; in New York the first German parish was founded in 1833. In fact, in every city where German Catholics settled, one of the first acts of the people was to organize a parish community. The same was true of all Catholic immigrant groups and this was why the national parish came into existence; rather than being organized territorially as was the custom in the Catholic church, immigrants in the United States were organized according to nationality or language. Oftentimes the organization of a benevolent society or a spiritual confraternity was the first step in the formation of a parish community.

The explicit purpose of the parish was religious; it enabled the people to hear sermons in their mother tongue, practice the devotions and customs of the old country, and raise their children in the faith of their ancestors. But in forming a benevolent society, raising money to buy land for a church, and building the church the people were also making a statement of who they were. They were defining their own identity as a people.

The formation of the parish school served a similar function. Its explicit purpose was education and among Catholic and Protestant immigrants, religious education as well. But the

---

[13]Quoted in *Berichte der Leopoldinen Stiftung*, Oct. 12, 1844.

school also helped to define the boundaries of the community and most importantly it sought to maintain this sense of identity over the generations.

It is also important to realize that in the process of forming local parish communities Catholic immigrants were intensifying their religious commitment. This is the second half of Smith's claim. An example from the Cincinnati German community underscores this point. In 1844 a group of German Catholics wanted to organize a new church in the city. Their first organizational meeting took place during the last week of October 1844 in a German church located in "Over the Rhine," the German section of the city. A building committee of ten laymen was chosen and they then proceeded to draft a constitution outlining the procedures for building the church. At another public meeting, German Catholics ratified the constitution and the establishment of St. John the Baptist parish was underway. The people purchased land for the church in the name of the bishop, John Purcell, and voted to name the church after his patron saint. Between October and March they held eight public meetings and voted upon such issues as the maximum price to be paid for the property, the number of doors in the church, the thickness of its walls and the size of its windows. As was true elsewhere, a collection committee organized at a public meeting solicited funds throughout the city for the church's construction.

On March 25, 1845 the laying of the cornerstone took place highlighted by an elaborate procession through "Over the Rhine." The people had planned the ceremony, procession, and accompanying festivities. Then in November of 1845 the dedication of the church took place. While all this was going on, the people also decided to build a school and, like the planning of the church, this "was agreed to and carried out with the accustomed meetings."[14]

[14]Joseph M. White, "Religion and Community: Cincinnati Germans 1814-1870" (Unpublished Ph.D. dissertation, University of Notre Dame, 1980), pp. 208-10.

Such intense involvement of Catholics in parish life became institutionalized in the lay trustee system whereby laymen elected by the people assisted in the government of the parish. Such involvement on the part of a significant number of immigrant Catholics strengthened their attachment to the church and intensified their commitment to religion. In fact, this attachment became so strong that in some instances the people would challenge priest and bishop in order to preserve the trustee system; some even appealed to the Pope and Vatican authorities before they would give up this type of involvement in their church.[15]

The involvement of the laity in the government of the local church by means of the lay trustee system was a theological statement as well. By this I mean that it was the concrete expression of an understanding of the church in which the laity had an important role. Such a model of the church was prevalent in the late eighteenth century and persisted throughout the nineteenth century. It would be erroneous to claim that this model of the church which emphasized the role of the laity in local church government was unique to the United States. It had European precedents throughout both the eighteenth and nineteenth centuries. But in the United States it ran head on into an opposite view of the church, namely the more hierarchical, clerical understanding in which the laity were left to pay, pray and obey. This hierarchical view of the church was gaining ascendancy in the second half of the century and became officially endorsed in the First Vatican Council in 1870. Because of the opposing and indeed threatening nature of the lay trustee concept of the church, both bishops and priests attacked it. It was too democratic and encouraged a dangerous spirit of independence. The conflict between these opposing views became quite bitter at times

[15]See Jay P. Dolan, *The American Catholic Experience: A History from Colonial Times to the Present* (New York, 1985),. pp. 158-194 for examples of such challenges.

precisely because more was at stake than just personalities. What was at stake was the choice between a clerical, monarchical model of the church or a more democratic, communal model in which the laity were involved in decision-making at the level of the local church.

Thus, the relationship between immigration and religion was threefold. In the first place, the immigrants identified themselves principally by means of their religious affiliation; we can call this the social aspect of this relationship. Secondly, the phenomenon of immigration provided the opportunity for the newcomers to intensify their religion and their attachment to the church; this can be labeled the religious aspect. Finally, the immigrant experience also had a theological aspect to it in that the organization of the local church inspired people to think about and understand the church in a particular manner.

Even though all immigrants did not have close ties to religion, those who did benefited from this relationship both socially and spiritually. Moreover, rather than being a secularizing process that weakened religion, immigration was a theologizing experience that transformed it.

Thus far I have emphasized lay involvement in the organization of the local church and its social, spiritual and theological aspects. By examining the religious world of the immigrants, their piety or spirituality if you wish, a similar three-dimensional relationship between religion and immigration emerges.

In examining the religious world of Catholic immigrants certain features stand out. In the first place, a very large number of the immigrants were not what can be called "Mass and sacraments Catholics." Studies of religious practice among various immigrant groups—Irish, Germans, Italians, Czechs, and Mexicans for example—demonstrate this. A large percentage of immigrants, 50 percent and better, were not accustomed to attending church and receiving the sacraments with any regularity and frequency. In the words of one contemporary observer, Orestes Brownson, Catholics "everywhere have ceased to receive the Sacraments, to attend Church, to say their prayers even; are profoundly ignorant of their religion, and completely indifferent to it, and are bringing up their families without any religion, except a remembrance that they have been baptized and call themselves Catholics."[16] Brownson's assessment was correct. Religious practice was low, indifferentism was widespread and the "loss of faith" was real. Secondly, the immigrants were arriving in a country where the Catholic church was institutionally underdeveloped; this was more true in the early nineteenth century than later, but even in the late nineteenth century when Catholic churches dotted the city landscape, the new immigrants—Italians, Mexicans, Polish and other Eastern European groups—found a church that was poorly prepared to receive them. Thirdly, the immigrants were settling in a country where there was a strong and developing tradition of religious freedom; this meant that as regards religion they could take it or leave it. This was quite different from the old world where for centuries church and state had been closely tied together both politically and geographically. In the new world there was no revered cultural tradition to force them to join a church; neither was the government inclined to coerce them to support a particular church.

Because of the atmosphere of freedom, the underdeveloped nature of the institutional church, and their low level of religious practice, Catholic immigrants were excellent candidates for a religious revival. The 1850s marked the beginnings of this revival crusade and the manner in which it was accomplished was through the parish mission. The parish mission was the Catholic counterpart to the Protestant revival and after the 1850s it became a standard feature of immigrant Catholicism well into the twentieth century. Year after year, preachers

[16]Quoted in Dolan, *Catholic Revivalism: The American Experience 1830-1900* (Notre Dame, In. 1978), p. 42.

mounted the pulpits of Catholic America and called the people to conversion. The people responded and through the sacraments of Penance and the Eucharist they revitalized their faith and strengthened their commitment to the church.

While this revival crusade was going on, immigrant Catholics were also experiencing a devotional revolution. Like the revival crusade the evidence for this is very convincing. Once again the 1850s marked the beginning of a new era. After 1850 the number of prayerbooks published in the United States increased substantially and even more significantly the number of devotions in these prayer books increased. After the 1850s the number of religious confraternities multiplied to the extent that these societies comprised 60 percent of all the parish societies organized in the second half of the nineteenth century. Much of this devotion centered on the saints, those heavenly aunts and uncles whom people called upon in times of need. The immigrants celebrated the feasts of the saints with great fervor and display. Every July, Italian areas in New York came alive with a weeklong celebration in honor of Our Lady of Mt. Carmel. Every December, the Feast of Our Lady of Guadalupe transformed Mexican barrios into open air cathedrals. People flocked to local shrines of individual saints associated with the healing powers of statues, relics or pictures; by 1900 at least eighteen such shrines existed and more were founded in the early twentieth century. Novenas were another popular expression of this devotional revolution and by the 1930s some churches were attracting thousands of people at their weekly novena services. The parochial school nurtured this piety by introducing the students to the celestial community of the saints and the elaborate network of devotions that brought these heavenly relatives into their lives.[17]

This devotional revolution not only transformed the environment of the school, but it also changed the way people

[17]See Dolan, *The American Catholic Experience*, pp. 211-219 and 234-235.

decorated their home. A social worker's description of the apartment of an Irish Catholic family revealed how elaborate and extensive such decoration could be:

> In the living and bedroom stands a large wooden wardrobe, which contains all the family clothes, treasures, cast-off clothing, etc. Next to this is the bureau. ... On the bureau is the family shrine, a brown wooden box with a slanting roof. In this there is an image of the Virgin, over whom is hung a rosary. The family Bible and a picture of St. Anthony are also placed on the bureau. On the mantle piece there are a brown wooden clock, several brightly colored vases filled with artificial flowers, two glass crucifixes, a china image of the Virgin, a plaster image of Mary with the Infant Jesus and some gaudy calendars. ... On the walls hang colored pictures of St. Benedict and Christ healing the sick, a newspaper print of Pope Leo XIII and of Pope Pius; a photograph of a family tombstone in Ireland; a color print of a praying child and several insurance, grocer, and brewery calendars. Over the mantle hangs a chromo of the father in a bright gilt frame decorated by palm leaves. On either side hang bright prints of saints, also a picture of a young woman and child under a shower of apple blossoms ... a door opens on the west side of this room to the smaller bedroom ... the walls are decorated with bright pictures of angels and saints.[18]

The Irish were not unique in this regard. Houses of other Catholics prominently displayed such religious symbols. Among Mexican Catholics it was even commonplace to have a small altar and shrine in the home where the family regularly prayed.

The growth and consolidation of this devotional revolution

---

[18]Elsa G. Herzfeld, *Family Monographs* (New York, 1905), pp. 45-46 and 15.

and its nurturing of a new style of religion in Catholic America was the most significant reform that took place in American Catholicism during the era of the immigrant church; and it ranks in significance with another period of reform, that of the post-Vatican II era of the 1960s and 70s.

By the early twentieth century it was clear that the mass of Catholics were more assiduous in practicing their religion. In the early nineteenth century priest confessors frequently remarked about the length of time people had been away from the sacraments of Penance and Communion; by the late nineteenth and early twentieth century such comments were rare. Catholics were more inclined now to make their Easter duty, that is receive Communion once a year during the Easter season. In the early decades of the nineteenth century churchgoers received Communion infrequently, but by the end of the century monthly communion had become the norm for these people; by the early twentieth century more frequent reception of communion even became popular. Revivals were frequent events in Catholic parishes and attendance at them was quite good. Prayerbooks, devotional pamphlets, novels, magazines and newspapers became commonplace in Catholic families. Catholic grammar schools and academies grew at a fast pace and they became culture factories for devotional Catholicism. Whether or not Catholics in 1900 were any more religious than Catholics in 1820 is hard to say. Most likely they were not. But they were practicing their religion much more— attending Mass more regularly, receiving Communion more frequently, and performing a greater variety of devotional rituals. A new culture of piety, devotional Catholicism, had developed and it not only reinforced American Catholicism, it also changed the way people thought.

This brings us to a second aspect of the relationship between religion and immigration, namely that it was a theologizing experience. In the very process of intensifying their religion and their commitment to the church, immigrant Catholics were also developing a specific theology or ethos.

In describing the way Catholics thought about themselves and the world in which they lived I want to focus on the central features of this mental landscape, those major land-marks which in towering over all else had a major influence in shaping the Catholic worldview. There were four such central traits—authority, sin, ritual, and the miraculous. Such concepts are found in other religious traditions as well since they are so fundamental to the Christian system of belief. Yet, within the Roman Catholic tradition they took on a special meaning and set Catholics apart from other people in the United States.

The nineteenth century was a time when the *authority* of the Catholic church was under siege; in reaction to this the church's authority was reasserted with excessive vigor. The highpoint of this crusade to strengthen the authority of the church was the declaration of papal infallibility in 1870 at the First Vatican Council. In the United States where the spirit of independence reigned supreme, it was especially imperative that the church assert its authority.

Within the immigrant community, loyalty to the Pope was emphasized and Pius IX became a very popular pope with the masses of the people. The local bishop shared in this emphasis on authority and the Third Baltimore Council in 1886 was a ringing affirmation of their authority in the church. The local pastor also benefited from this and he became the chief author-ity figure in the local church. One immigrant pastor, Vincent Barzynski, in a very succinct explanation of the basis for a pastor's authority, captured the essence of the hierarchical model of government operative in the Catholic church:

> If you desire to work in the name of God, pay heed to the words of Christ, because God the Father gave us only one Christ; if you wish to labor for Christ, then listen to Peter, for Christ gave us only one Peter; if you want to work in Peter's name, obey the Pope, because he is the only true successor to the first Pope; if you wish to work in the Pope's name, obey the bishop, because only the bishop rules the

diocese; if you wish to obey the bishop, then you must obey
your pastor, for the bishop gave you only one pastor.[19]

Another way in which authority shaped the Catholic mind
was through church laws, those rules and regulations that
seemed to pop up everywhere. First there were the church
commandments such as attending church on Sunday and holy
days and going to confession and communion once a year.
Invested with the church's authority, they assumed the gravity
and importance of the biblical commandments. In addition,
there was the body of legislation that American bishops enacted during the course of the nineteenth century. The hierarchy was anxious to establish discipline in the Catholic community and they passed a wide variety of laws to do this.
These ranged from outlawing membership in such secret societies as the Oddfellows to prescribing the proper form of
clerical dress. Finally, in 1917 a new Code of Canon Law was
promulgated for Catholics throughout the world. A major
overhaul of church laws, its publication spawned a cottage
industry of canon lawyers with their commentaries, books,
and journals.

Raised in such a culture of authority, Catholics were taught
to be docile and submissive. The most persuasive image used
to cultivate such docility was that of Jesus, the suffering Savior.
Evoked to persuade others to follow his example, the image
portrayed was one of docile obedience; indeed, Jesus was
obedient even unto death. Absent from this portrait were any
signs of independence or rebellion. Obedience and docility,
not dissent and independence, were the ideals cherished in the
Catholic community. Clearly this did not mean that all were
submissive servants. Trustee conflicts, parish wars, and church
schisms were a fact of life in immigrant Catholicism. Yet, as

[19]Quoted in John Joseph Parot, *The Polish Catholics in Chicago* 1850-1920 (DeKalb, Illinois 1981), p. 124.

the authoritarian culture of devotional Catholicism strengthened its grip on people, obedience rather than rebellion became the standard. The emergence of clerical control by the early twentieth century was a good indicator of how strong this mentality had become. People could and did rebel, but such dissent became more isolated and more private. More common was the attitude expressed by a French Canadian immigrant. Speaking about the practice of birth control among Catholics she observed that "most of the French people were not rebellious in any way.... They were people with a deep, simple, religious faith."[20] In a culture of authority simple meant docile.

A second dominant trait of devotional Catholicism was its emphasis on *sin*. This was rooted in the early centuries of the church when the tradition of St. Augustine became so influential in shaping the religious world of Catholics. The Augustinian tradition espoused a very pessimistic concept of the human person. Original sin had undermined the strength of men and women and made them victims of sin. Gifted with freedom but bewitched by sin, men and women had to struggle to attain holiness on earth and salvation afterwards. In some religious traditions, the Calvinist being the most notable, salvation was reserved for a chosen few, the elect of God. For others, Catholics among them, holiness and salvation was open to all, but you had to earn it; the way you did this was through a victorious struggle over sin. Since the human person was so inclined to evil, however, people needed a great deal of assistance in their battle against sin.

Because sin was so pervasive and powerful the evil inclinations of people had to be curbed. The way this was done was through a multitude of laws and regulations which helped to discipline and strengthen Catholics in their struggle against sin. The church with its culture of authority as well as its

---

[20]Quoted in Tamara K. Hareven and Randolph Langenbach, *Amoskeag* (New York, 1978), p. 257.

sacramental system became a necessary companion in this struggle. In other words, a culture of sin demanded a culture of authority.

The evidence for this is quite convincing. Saturday afternoons and evenings, crowds of people created long lines at confession, so long that priests and people alike complained about them. Prayerbooks devoted an inordinate amount of space to sin and confession. The parish mission put a special emphasis on sin and conversion, and terrifying sermons on hell became a tradition in the immigrant church.

A specifically Catholic trait in the economy of sin was the element of mercy and forgiveness guaranteed at confession. Sin may have been deadly and guilt may have been intense, but the "waters of grace" washed it all away and restored the sinner to virtue and life. This indeed was an important part of the Catholic theological system and it clearly tempered the harshness of the culture of sin.

Not all Catholics accepted the culture of sin and authority. Some rebelled against priest and bishop; many never went to church on a regular basis; mixed marriages did occur; and men continued to frequent the saloon. That is not the point, however. The standard was there to follow and the culture was present to form you, and growing up Catholic in the era of the immigrant church meant that a person had to cope with a culture built on sin and sustained by authority. You could resist and rebel, as many did, but even in your resistance the culture pursued you like Francis Thompson's "Hound of Heaven," never letting you forget what you were fleeing.

A third dominant feature of devotional Catholicism was its emphasis on *ritual*. The celebration of the Mass and the sacraments were the principal rituals for most immigrant Catholics. In addition, there was a myriad of devotional rituals; some were public but most were private. Few of these rituals were new to the nineteenth century. They were traditional Catholic practices which had been revived with great vigor during the devotional revolution of the nineteenth century.

New papal indulgences attached to these devotions made them especially appealing and their popularity kept an entire industry of religious publishers and merchants in business.

All religions emphasize the importance of ritual, but for some it is clearly more central to their identity. This was certainly true of devotional Catholicism. Religion was associated with the performance of certain external acts. The divine was accessible only through ritual—that was clearly the message conveyed. It may not have been completely orthodox, but the centrality of ritual in devotional Catholicism clearly suggested that it was the popular, working theology of both priests and people. The importance of the priest and the church in this culture was clear. Without the priest the critical public rituals could not be performed; as regards the extensive world of private ritual, to be effective they had to be performed as the church instructed and indulgences could only be achieved after a prescribed ritual within the ritual had been completed. For these reasons the ritual culture enhanced the culture of authority and made the church and its hierarchical system all the more essential to devotional Catholicism.

The fourth and final trait of devotional Catholicism was its openness to the *miraculous*. A sense of mystery, a sense of the holy, was part of the mystical tradition of Roman Catholicism. Identified closely with the monastic way of life and certain saints, it also found a niche among the common people. The celebration of Mass certainly evoked this atmosphere of the holy as did the numerous religious processions in and about the church and neighborhood. But even more telling was the popular belief in miraculous cures. Part of the cultural baggage that Catholics brought with them was an attachment to a non-Christian, religious culture. Distinct from the official religion of the church it was the realm of folk tales and magic, banshees and charms, a supernatural world of good and evil forces. Catholicism, with its elaborate network of saints, its use of sacred objects such as relics, rosaries, candles, scapulars, and holy water, and its emphasis on the need for ritual to bridge the chasm between the human and divine, blended in nicely with this folk religion. Rather than try to abolish such deep-seated cultural beliefs the church sought to channel them into its official network of prayer and worship. The result was a curious blend of both official and folk beliefs and practices.

A study done of the Irish living on Manhattan's West Side at the turn of the century uncovered widespread belief in the supernatural powers of scapulars, charms, and relics as well as certain folk practices associated with birth and marriage. The Irish tradition of the festive wake was another example of the persistence of folk religious beliefs despite prolonged opposition on the part of church authorities.[21] Marriage among Hispanic Catholics mixed together Hispanic and Anglo, folk and institutional religious customs. Belief in a supernatural world of the spirit beyond the realm of the official church was commonplace among Italians.

The fascination with the miraculous was a distinctive trait of devotional Catholicism. The Catholic God was a personal figure who listened to the prayers of people and acted on their behalf. God was not some distant, disinterested force but one who would reach down and touch the lives of the people. The saints were frequently called on to persuade God to act and such successful intervention understandably made them very popular among the people. The linking of such temporal favors as health, personal safety, and individual success with the rituals of devotional Catholicism was another major reason for the popularity of these devotions among the people. This was especially true when dramatic cures or healings took place in association with the performance of certain devotions such as prayers at a Marian shrine or the shrine of some saint. The reporting of such miracles was commonplace and such news served to enhance the popularity of these shrines and devotions.[22]

---

[21]Dolan, *The American Catholic Experience*, p. 234.

[22]*Ibid.*, pp. 234-235.

The God of devotional Catholicism was a God of many faces. He was a lawmaker who exercised his authority through a myriad of rules established by the church which Jesus founded. Clearly an authoritarian figure, He punished sinners severely through the everlasting pains of hell. Yet, another side of Him was more benign. In His mercy He would forgive repentant sinners, cure the sick and heal the lame. Other cultures in other times represented God in different ways, but for devotional Catholics He was both stern judge and kind father. This is what made Him at once so fearsome and attractive, dreaded and loved. A culture of authority and sin emphasized the dark side of the divine while the practice of ritual and belief in the miraculous underscored the bright side.

The emphasis on authority, sin, ritual and the miraculous shaped the way immigrant Catholics thought about themselves; another way of putting this is that the practice of religion in the immigrant community was a theologizing experience.

The third and final aspect of the relationship between religion and immigration was what I have labeled the social dimension, or the need for the newcomers to define who they were. Just as the organization of the local parish enabled the immigrants to establish a focal point of their identity in the new world, so also the articulation and practice of a specific religion or spirituality became a mark of identity in the religiously pluralistic American society. In the United States religious freedom was a way of life. This meant that as many religions as the people wanted would be able to compete in the market place. Such competition not only nurtured division, but it also meant that each group had to define itself clearly so that its identity would be recognizable in the midst of the religious market place. The segregation of urban America along racial, ethnic, and class lines meant that Catholics lived in neighborhood cultural ghettos separated from the rest of society. Even in small rural towns where many Catholics lived, such social and residential segregation was common; towns were either preponderantly Catholic in population or if not,

were often so geographically divided that Catholics lived seg-
regated from Protestants. In such a social situation Catholic
outsiders needed to acquire an identity. They were newcomers
and the history and lore of the American past was foreign to
them; unlike their experience in the Old World they did not
have a tradition or an *ancient regime* to identify with. Devotional Catholicism thus became a means of social identity; it
gave people a specifically Catholic identity in a Protestant
society. Certainly ethnicity or one's nationality was a vital
trademark with which first and second generation immigrants
identified. But religion was such an essential part of ethnic
identity that in the United States religious affiliation became
the "organizing impulse" among immigrants. Moreover, in the
United States, a society that still strongly believed in religion
as a major element in the American way of life, religious
identity was especially meaningful and valuable.

It is clear that the experience of immigration had a decisive
impact on religion. Rather than disappearing the religion of
the old world acquired new strength in the new world. The
relationship between religion and the people was altered as
they intensified their religious commitment and redefined their
identity as a people set apart. In the process they also articulated a theology, an ethos if you wish, that took on a special
meaning in the immigrant community.

Our immigrant ancestors have passed on to us a valuable
legacy, a living faith, and we should recall the people whose
faith and commitment turned the dreams of a few into a
reality for thousands. Historians are fond of pointing out the many
colleges founded in colonial times and concluding how literate
and cultured the Puritans and their descendants were. It is
equally true that in the nineteenth century virtually every
Catholic immigrant community established its own college.
These institutions, stand as a testimony to the culture and
values of the immigrants.

From Church-State to Religion and Politics: The Case of the U.S. Catholic Bishops

J. Bryan Hehir, Th.D
U.S. Catholic Conference
and
Kennedy Institute of Ethics
Washington, D.C.

A *New York Times* Sunday magazine cover story in August 1984 was entitled "America's Activist Bishops." Depending upon the reader's theological and/or political orientation, the title was either an indictment or a compliment. In either case the term "activist" only partially communicated the meaning of a complex phenomenon. It is the theological and political foundations of the activism of the U.S. Bishops which this paper seeks to analyze. Twenty years ago no analyst would have used "activist" to describe the Catholic hierarchy in the United States. But by the mid-1980s the notion of "activist bishops" was solidly established in the public mind and it was tied to a series of positions the Catholic bishops had taken in the national policy debate.

On four issues which had been at the center of the political agenda in the United States for a decade, the Catholic bishops, acting through their national organization, the U.S. Catholic Conference (USCC), had staked out detailed positions, rooted in a religious-moral tradition,[1] but related to specific dimensions of the public policy debate. The four issues were: abortion, nuclear strategy, equity in the economy, and U.S. policy in Central America.

For each of the four issues the bishops had used a different method of communicating their position to the church and the wider society. From the time of the 1973 Supreme Court decision on abortion, the bishops took a strong public stand of advocacy for the right to life of the unborn. The position has been expressed in numerous congressional testimonies and statements of the episcopal leadership as well as in an extensive "respect life" parish education program which is sponsored nationally by the bishops. To address the nuclear issue the bishops established a special committee (chaired by Cardinal Bernardin) charged with drafting a pastoral letter, *The Challenge of Peace: God's Promise and Our Response*. A similar process has been used to draft another pastoral letter on *Catholic Social Teaching and the U.S. Economy*; the special committee for this letter was chaired by Archbishop Weakland of Milwaukee. The bishops' position on Central America has been expressed in annual testimony before the Congress every year since 1980. Each of the four positions has had a distinctive impact—often with different groups, but collectively they have established the bishops as a voice in the national public debate. One characteristic of their presence in the debate is the range of the issues addressed. Few, if any, other national organizations join the bishops' position on abortion with their kind of critique of nuclear

---

[1]There is no one place to find all the positions; the best source is *Origins*, the documentary service of the U.S. Catholic Conference, published on a weekly basis.

policy or their critique of U.S. policy in Central America.[2]

It is precisely the scope of the bishops' concerns and the increasing intensity with which they have taken part in the public debate which makes it useful to step back from any single position and explore the premises of their public activity. This paper will probe the premises in terms of three questions. First, the constitutional question: whether the activism of a religious organization accords with the constitutional system of the United States. Second, the theological question: what is the theological basis for the social involvement of the church? Third, the pastoral-political question: how do the bishops function within the public arena? By using these questions it will be possible to examine the bishops as pastors applying a religious-moral tradition to political questions and as public actors seeking to shape and influence the debate and decision-making of a pluralist society.

To summarize the paper, I will contend that the U.S. Bishops' constitutional position is American, their theological vision is Catholic and their pastoral-political style is democratic. In arguing these three propositions, I will join the positions of the bishops to key themes which form the basis of their activity, but often are not known in the wider public discussion.

I. The Constitutional Question: An American Response

The constitutional question is usually posed in terms of "the separation of church and state." The phrase is omnipresent in American political discourse: it is the tag line for editorial writers, the way in which "the religious

---

[2]Cardinal Bernardin has tried to highlight the scope and connections of several issues in his "consistent ethic" addresses; cf *The Seamless Garment*, National Catholic Reporter Publishing Co., Kansas City, MO, 1984.

issue" is discussed in political campaigns and the shorthand used by plain citizens to define the relationship of religion and politics. The phrase refers to the First Amendment of the Constitution. Strictly speaking, the "separation clause" is not literally found in the First Amendment, but the idea of "separation" has served to structure the understanding of the role of the church in the political process.

In the face of "activism" by the largest single religious denomination in the country, the constitutional question inevitably arises. Does such activism breach the separation of church and state? Is it appropriate legally and politically? When faced with this question the U.S. Bishops have responded with a blend of Catholic theology and American political theory. Their response to the constitutional question involves three steps.

First, a working definition of the political meaning of the First Amendment; essentially it says that religious organizations should expect neither favoritism nor discrimination in the exercise of their civil or religious responsibilities. It is important to stress that the separation clause is meant to protect against both favoritism or discrimination. There is little or no indication in law, history or policy that silencing the religious voices of the nation was the intent of the First Amendment. Given this definition of the meaning of separation the Catholic response is to agree with it.

It is necessary to say that Catholic theology today is much clearer in its response than it would have been before the Second Vatican Council. In the period between the Reformation and Vatican II, the church affirmed the moral desirability of "a Catholic state" in cases where the majority of the population was Catholic. In the nineteenth century, the First Vatican Council (1870) modified this teaching by distinguishing between "The Thesis" or normative case of a Catholic state and "The Hypothesis"—the exceptional case which is tolerated because seeking to achieve a "Catholic state" would cause more harm than good.

It was precisely the achievement of Vatican II's *Declaration on Religious Liberty* to replace the normative status of the Catholic state with the principle that all the church expects from the political authority in society is the freedom to fulfill its ministry. The argument of the conciliar document which led to this conclusion brought the church to accept religious pluralism as the context of its ministry (i.e., not something to be simply resisted, but a challenge to be worked with), to accept the constitutional or limited state as the best safeguard of political liberty and freedom as the principle of political organization which is most conducive to protecting the basic rights of the person. Each of these points had a disputed history in Catholic theology and the acceptance of them as part of the conciliar declaration constituted a major theoretical development in Catholic theology.[3] In practical terms it supports the bishops' acceptance of the separation clause; acceptance is possible because the church should expect freedom, not favoritism, in the public arena.

Second, the acceptance of the separation of church and state is to be understood—politically and theologically—in light of the distinction between society and the state. Accepting the separation of church and state should not be understood to mean accepting the separation of the church from society. Central to the notion of democratic policy is the distinction of society and state; the state is only part of society—to fail to make this distinction leads to a totalitarian notion of the state. The church-state relationship is a crucial but narrowly defined question; it governs the juridical relationship of the institution of the church to the institution of the state. But beyond this relationship there exists a whole range of issues governing the church's presence in the wider society. The activity of the

[3]For a survey of this history see J.C. Murray, "The Problem of Religious Freedom," *Theological Studies*, 25 (1964) p. 518 ff.

bishops on nuclear policy or abortion is often directed toward policies which are set by the state, but their involvement in these issues occurs in and through the channels a democratic society provides for public debate.

Third, in locating the role of the church in the wider societal framework it is useful to revert to another key category in Western political thought, voluntary associations. Like the distinction between society and state, voluntary associations are central features of a democratic polity. They exist to provide a buffer between the state and the citizen, and they also provide structured organizations which have the capacity to influence the polity and policies of society. In the American political system, the church is a voluntary association. While this is not an adequate theological understanding of the church, it does provide a sociological description of how the church shares certain characteristics with other voluntary associations.

Voluntary associations encompass professional, cultural and labor organizations; they bring different contributions to the public arena usually linked to the specific issues which interest them. The church should bring a systematic capability to raise and address the moral dimensions of public issues and it also brings the capability to engage the members of its constituency in public discussion about these issues. In writing the two pastoral letters, the bishops made it clear that they were addressing two audiences: the community of the church and the wider civil community. Precisely as a voluntary association the church is situated to join the public debate in this dual fashion.

To provide this interpretation of the constitutional response of the U.S. Bishops is to see their dependence not only on Vatican II but also on the theology of the late John Courtney Murray, S.J. (d. 1967). Murray was the principal architect of *The Declaration on Religious Liberty*. This was a fitting tribute to the man whose previous twenty years of theological research had made possible the step taken at the Council.

In developing his theology of church and state, Murray

examined at length a series of questions which bear directly on the public ministry of the U.S. Bishops today. The basic lines of Murray's work can only be identified here and then referred to in other parts of this paper.[4] Murray's fundamental contribution was to provide the moral foundations of the church's recognition of religious liberty as a human right. He joined this with a theological case for the church's acceptance of democracy as it had emerged since the eighteenth century. Both of these themes are found in the Vatican statement on religious freedom. In addition Murray articulated a political philosophy concerning the moral foundations of a secular pluralist democracy and how the Catholic church could play a positive role in American society.

Murray's position was never a facile call for accepting democracy without critique, much less endorsing dominant aspects of American society without question. He believed Catholic moral teaching and social philosophy provided the resources for a fundamental review of democratic polity and policies. But such a review should begin with a recognition of the common ground the church shared with the fruits of the democratic revolutions of the eighteenth century. For Murray the church in the United States had something to offer the universal church by sharing its experience of democratic polity, and he believed the church could serve civil society by a process of critical dialogue about public philosophy and public policies in the United States.

The separation of church and state—the constitutional question properly defined—provides a starting point for this critical dialogue. In exercising an activist social ministry, the bishops are endorsing the terms of the church-state provisions and accepting their role as participants in the church-society dialogue.

[4]In addition to the article in footnote 3, cf "The Issue of Church and State at Vatican II" *Theological Studies*, 27 (1966) pp. 580-606; *We Hold These Truths* (N.Y. Sheed and Ward, 1960); D. Pellotte, *John Courtney Murray: Theologian In Conflict* (N.Y.: Paulist Press, 1976).

II. The Theological Question: A Catholic Response

The source of the constitutional question is usually outside the community of the church; it most often arises from those who fear that an "activist church" will threaten the delicate constitutional fabric of a religiously pluralist society.

The source of the theological question is usually within the church itself; it arises from those who fear that an activist posture will corrupt the religious ministry of the church. Hence, the theological question usually asks what is the basis in Catholic teaching for an activist social role. The response which the bishops give to this question is crucial; failure to establish the theological legitimacy of their public activity can undercut them in the church and in society. For this reason, the bishops have responded in some detail to the theological question. Essentially the response has been to describe the activity of the episcopal conference as an extension and application of the social teaching of the universal church. This theme is found in both of the pastoral letters and in major addresses of the presidents of the episcopal conference over the last several years.[5]

The social teaching of the church has a long and complex history. As Ernst Troeltsch and others have documented, the Catholic church has always been a public church.[6] In the mid-nineteenth century the public ministry of the church was substantially expanded to address the consequences of the Industrial Revolution.

Beginning with the first of the "social encyclicals," Leo XIII's *Rerum Novarum* (1891), and extending through the most

---

[5]Cf. *The Challenge of Peace: God's Promise and Our Response* (Washington: USCC, 1983) esp. Introduction and Part One; "Catholic Social Teaching and the U.S. Economy," *Origins*, 14, #22-23, (Nov. 15, 1984). Bishop James Malone, Intersection of Public Opinion and Public Policy, *Origins*, 14, #24 (Nov. 29, 1984) p. 386 ff.

[6]E.Troeltsch, *The Social Teaching of the Christian Church* (N.Y.: Harper and Row, 1960) vol. I & II.

recent social teaching, John Paul II's *Laborem Exercens* (1981), the church developed a detailed commentary on the major socio-economic themes of the industrial and post-industrial ages.[7] This social teaching is the background for much of what the U.S. Bishops say in their pastoral on the economy. But it is the teaching of Vatican II which has provided a more comprehensive framework for social ministry and has served as the catalyst for the post-conciliar positions of the U.S. Bishops.

The Second Vatican Council was an event of systemic significance in the Catholic church; it also had distinct regional and local consequences. The intellectual and organizational implications of the Council are still being worked out. The systemic meaning of the Council is contained in the sixteen documents it produced.[8] Like the *Declaration on Religious Liberty*, many of the conciliar texts constituted a major development in Catholic theology. This was the case for the *Dogmatic Constitution on the Church*, the *Decree on Ecumenism* and the *Dogmatic Constitution on Divine Revelation*. But no document from Vatican II was more of an indication of development in the tradition than the *Pastoral Constitution on the Church in the Modern World*.

While most of the other sixteen documents of the Council had been planned before its first meeting, there had been no plan to produce a text on the relationship of the church to the world. It was believed adequate to describe the church's ministry in the *Constitution on the Church*. But that text focused almost exclusively on the internal life of the church. It was precisely the experience of the Council fathers, particularly when they were busy discussing the nature and mission of the church, that they became convinced of the need for a separate,

---

[7]For a summary of the key documents cf J. Gremillion, *The Gospel of Peace and Justice* (N.Y.: Orbis Books, 1979).

[8]There are several collections of the conciliar texts. Cf A. Flannery, O.P., ed., *Vatican Council II: The Conciliar and Post-Conciliar Documents* (Collegeville: The Liturgical Press, 1975).

in-depth theological treatment of the church's relationship to the world. The eventual product, the *Pastoral Constitution on the Church in the Modern World*, is the longest and many would say the single most influential document of Vatican II.

An illustration of the impact of the *Pastoral Constitution* can be found in the regional consequences it has produced. The years since the Council have seen an intensified social ministry in the church throughout the world. Two examples of this general trend are the consequences of the *Pastoral Constitution* in Latin America and in the United States. The bishops of Latin America systematically applied the conciliar vision of Vatican II to their regional pastoral setting through the Medellin Conference (1968) and the Puebla Conference (1979). Most noticeable in this process of pastoral renewal has been the positions of the church on issues of social justice and human rights. While the theological vision which has energized this transformation has its own local roots, character and architects, the pervasive influence of the *Pastoral Constitution* stands behind the Latin American church.

In the United States, at least in the engagement of the hierarchy, the influence of the *Pastoral Constitution* is even more evident. The first contribution of the document has been to establish a solidly grounded consensus among the bishops about the meaning and importance of social ministry. The "social teaching" of the popes had provided a detailed moral framework, but it lacked a clear ecclesiological foundation and articulation of the centrality of social ministry for the church. The significance of having an episcopal consensus about the social ministry is that it allows the bishops to debate and differ on concrete issues in the socio-political-economic order without placing in doubt the need for the church to be deeply involved in these questions. The consensus, built on the conciliar teaching, provides a legitimation of and a foundation for the social ministry and grounds the public ministry of the episcopal conference.

But the significance of the *Pastoral Constitution* is not

exhausted by its contribution to a general perspective on social ministry. Using the peace pastoral as an example, it is possible to see how the theology of the conciliar text specifically shaped the teaching of the U.S. Bishops. It is difficult to imagine the bishops of the United States issuing their pastoral letter in 1983 if they had not been schooled in the ecclesiology of the *Pastoral Constitution* for the last eighteen years. There are three aspects of the theology of the *Pastoral Constitution* which prepared for the pastoral letter: 1) its definition of the *place* of the church in the world; 2) its description of the church's *presence* in the world; and 3) its *perspective* on the church's teaching style.

The *Pastoral Constitution* provides the most comprehensive statement in modern times of the church's *place* in the world. The conciliar document is not content either with homiletic statements that the church should be active in the affairs of the world, or even with a repetition of previous moral teaching on specific social questions. Rather, the distinctive contribution of the conciliar text is that it provides a theological rationale for the entire social ministry of the church.

Noticeably absent, even in the best of the social encyclicals, has been an explicit discussion of how the social vision is related to a theological understanding of the church's nature and mission. The gap has been an ecclesiological one, a failure to join the activity of the church in the world to the inner nature of the church. The lack of such a statement has the effect of leaving the valuable social tradition at the edge of the church's life; it resides there as an aspect of the church's ministry but not a central focus of its life.

The *Pastoral Constitution* establishes an explicit theological relationship between the moral vision of Catholic social teaching and its ecclesiological significance. The linkage is made in two steps.

First, the *Pastoral Constitution* takes the key concept from the social teaching and describes the church's role in society in light of it. The church, says the conciliar text, "is at once the sign and the safeguard of the transcendental dimension of the human person."[9] In this passage the tasks of protecting human dignity and promoting human rights take on ecclesial significance. They are not purely "secular" functions toward which the church is benignly but distantly disposed. Rather, the *Pastoral Constitution* calls the church to place itself in support of these tasks in every political system. The engagement of the Catholic church, as an institution and a community, in defense of human rights in political cultures as diverse as Poland, Brazil, South Africa, and South Korea testify to the impact of this linkage of moral teaching on human rights and the ecclesial teaching on the ministry of the church.

Second, the authors of the conciliar text recognized that it was insufficient to leave the theological argument at the point of linking the moral and the ecclesial themes. For as soon as the church takes this linkage seriously and engages in a consistent pursuit of human rights, the question which inevitably arises is whether such activity is beyond the scope of its competence or involves a politicization of religion. The deeper issue which needed to be addressed, therefore, was how the church influences the socio-political order without itself becoming politicized. This is the theological question in its most delicate form.

The response of the *Pastoral Constitution*, found in paragraphs 40-42, is clear and basic. The place of the church in the socio-political order is shaped by the following principles: a) the ministry of the church is religious in nature, it has no specifically political charism; b) the religious ministry has as its primary object the achievement of the Kingdom of God—the church is in a unique way the "instrument" of the Kingdom in history; c) the power of the Kingdom is designed to permeate every dimension of life; d) as the church pursues its properly religious ministry, it contributes to four areas of life which

[9]*The Pastoral Constitution*, #76 in Gremillion and Flannery, cited.

have direct social and political consequences; e) these four religiously rooted but politically significant goals are: 1) the defense of human dignity; 2) the promotion of human rights; 3) the cultivation of the unity of the human family; and 4) the provision of meaning to every aspect of human activity.[10]

In the theology of the *Pastoral Constitution* the *place* of the church in the world is set by two principles: transcendence and compenetration. On the one hand the church, because its religious ministry transcends every political system, cannot be identified with or contained within any one political system. On the other hand, the church, precisely in pursuit of its religious ministry—adequately defined—should be engaged in the daily life of every socio-political entity. The engagement is "indirect," i.e., through the pursuit of the four goals outlined above; this form of witnessing to the life of the Kingdom in history is what John Courtney Murray called the principle of "compenetration."[11]

Examination of the place of the church in the world led the *Pastoral Constitution* to discuss the mode of the church's *presence* in the world. The church must contribute to each and every political system in a manner which preserves its identity and still makes an effective contribution to a just and peaceful society. The style of presence outlined in the *Pastoral Constitution* is the method of dialogue: "And so the Council, as witness and guide to the faith of the whole people of God, gathered together by Christ, can find no more eloquent expression of its solidarity and respectful affection for the whole human family to which it belongs, than to enter into dialogue with it about all these different problems."[12]

The *Pastoral Constitution* describes the attitude which the church brings to this dialogue with the world: the church has

---

[10]*Ibid.*, #40.

[11]Murray, *The Issue of Church and State at Vatican II*, p. 600.

[12]*The Pastoral Constitution*, #3.

something to learn and something to teach. In a spirit strikingly different from that of the eighteenth and nineteenth centuries, the church acknowledges its need for and its desire to draw upon the various disciplines and areas of expertise which contribute to the building of contemporary society. In a major teaching document of the Council, the bishops committed themselves to a teaching style which seeks a precise understanding of contemporary problems in all their complexity prior to making moral judgments or providing religious guidance about these questions.

The willingness to learn from the world is partly motivated by the desire of the church to contribute to a deeper sense of the human and religious significance of contemporary life. While the *Pastoral Constitution* exhibits an attractive modesty in the face of secular complexity, the Council was not paralyzed by the data of the empirical sciences. The pastoral desire to dialogue moves beyond listening to that of interpreting: "The church likewise believes that the key, the center and the purpose of the whole of man's history is to be found in its Lord and Master.... And that is why the Council, relying on the inspiration of Christ, ... proposes to speak to all men in order to unfold the mystery that is man and cooperate in tackling the main problems facing the world today."[13] At the heart of the dense technical complexity of the age lie problems of meaning, purpose and moral direction.

The method of dialogue has been a central characteristic in the preparation of both the peace pastoral and the economic pastoral. The Bernardin Committee, for example, followed the style of *Pastoral Constitution* by first listening and then speaking. The first year of the Committee's work was largely given over to a series of "hearings" in which a number of people were invited before the Committee to share their expertise and experiences.

[13]*Ibid.*, #10.

The "witnesses" included a panel of biblical scholars, a dozen moralists of differing persuasions, a spectrum of arms control experts, two former Secretaries of Defense, a physician, two retired military officers, a panel of peace activists and specialists in nonviolent defense and conflict resolution. The hearing process closed with a full day of discussion with representatives of the Reagan Administration: the Secretary of Defense, the Undersecretary of State for Political Affairs and the Director of the Arms Control and Disarmament Agency. Through these hearings the bishops were immersed in the problems of nuclear strategy, arms control and the likely consequences of a nuclear war.

The process of dialogue extended to the whole bishops' conference when the various drafts of the pastoral letter were published for analysis and debate. The scope of the dialogue and the degree of detail the Committee addressed went beyond that used in the *Pastoral Constitution*, but the method of dialogue was drawn from the conciliar experience.

The dialogue was carried on within the *perspective* of the *Pastoral Constitution*. That perspective is expressed in the following passage from the document: "At all times the church carries the responsibility of reading the signs of the times and of interpreting them in the light of the Gospel. . . . " The biblical phrase "signs of the times" points toward a methodological principle of the *Pastoral Constitution*. It means beginning the process of theological analysis with a concrete examination of the nature of the questions to be addressed, then moving to a theological reflection on the major characteristics of the problem.

The American pastoral letter began with an assessment of the "New Moment" in the nuclear age. The bishops sought first to understand the content and dynamics of this "New Moment" prior to making their contribution to it. They went on in the letter to assess the *nature* of deterrence as a predominant sign of the times before they tried to make a *moral* judgment on the policy of deterrence.

On all three of these ecclesiological themes, the place of the church in the world, its style of presence and its perspective, the contributions of the *Pastoral Constitution* directly shaped how the American bishops pursued their task.

In this sense the U.S. Bishops represent the Catholic theological response, but they have also shaped this universal teaching to fit the secular pluralistic and democratic character of the pastoral setting in which they minister.

III. The Pastoral-Political Question: A "Democratic" Response

The adaptation of the Catholic theological tradition to the dynamic of the American political process involves an act of creative pastoral leadership by the U.S. Bishops. A text which has guided their pastoral work for the last fifteen years is the following statement of Pope Paul VI:

> In the face of such widely varying situations it is difficult for us to utter a unified message and to put forward a solution which has universal validity. Such is not our ambition, nor is it our mission. It is up to the Christian communities to analyze with objectivity the situation which is proper to their own country, to shed on it the light of the gospel's unalterable words and to draw principles of reflection, norms of judgment and directives for action from the social teaching of the Church.[14]

The text was an explicit recognition by the pope that a church with a worldwide constituency and a universal message is in need of creative shaping of the vision to make it real, relevant and effective to quite different situations. The "local

---

[14]Paul VI, *The Eightieth Year*, #4, in Gremillion, cited.

church" is an actor in the social ministry. The task of a local episcopal conference is not simply to receive from Rome, but also to assess the specific dimensions of its cultural, political, economic system. It is one thing to teach the social vision in an authoritarian regime of the right (much of Latin America), another thing to witness in an equally repressive regime of the left (most of Eastern Europe) and something quite different to influence a secular, democratic, religiously pluralist culture like the United States.

When the U.S. Bishops try to influence this specific cultural setting, they reflect the influence of two forces: the general style of Catholic social teaching which has traditionally been sensitive to the need to translate a religious vision in a world of many faiths and no faith; and the insight of Murray's work on the role of the church in a democracy.

Troeltsch's classic study on the social teaching of the churches highlighted the Catholic conviction that faith *and* reason, the church *and* the world were complementary, not in radical contradiction. This conception of faith and the role of the church shaped the social teaching in the direction of joining the revelation of the Scriptures with the philosophy of natural law. The function of the natural law social ethic in the Catholic tradition is to provide a philosophical framework to relate the general themes of revelation to the complexity and contingency of changing historical situations, and also to mediate the religiously based tradition for a pluralistic culture. From the bishops' arguments in defense of the rights of the unborn, to their human rights analysis of U.S. policy in Central America, to their just-war critique of nuclear policy, the Catholic leadership has tried to play this mediating role between faith and culture, between church and society. On all these issues there has been a conscious effort by the bishops not to adopt a sectarian posture. They have maintained this position often in spite of criticism from quarters within the church who want a "stronger" or more "evangelical" emphasis, less open to the balancing of various claims and less concerned about shaping the teaching in a manner accessible to those outside the community of faith.

In taking this position of a public church the bishops are not only continuing a general characteristic of the Catholic tradition, they are also following Murray's conception of the role of the church in a pluralist democracy. Murray was convinced that such a polity cannot survive in a moral vacuum. Since the very basis of a religiously pluralist society involves disagreement on fundamental questions, Murray believed that a moral consensus, narrowly drawn but critically important in its substance, had to be shaped which could give direction to public policy. Murray was both modest and precise in his expectations about such a moral consensus.[15] On one hand, he believed it could not encompass every moral issue facing society, but only those with direct bearing on the public order. On the other hand, he was convinced that some consensus had to be widely held on public order questions. The public agenda of the 1980s—from nuclear weapons to medical technology— illustrates the validity of Murray's concern about a moral consensus. Moral issues are at the heart of public policy—few dispute the point. But recognition of the point does not supply moral direction; it only initiates the search for moral wisdom.

Murray never believed that a single religious community could be the guardian of the moral consensus. He saw the church, the academy and other key institutions in society as co-responsible for carrying on the continuous public dialogue needed to shape a moral framework for policy.

This conception of the role of the religious community is prominent in both of the pastoral letters. To use the peace pastoral again as an example:

> As bishops we believe that the nature of Catholic moral teaching, the principles of Catholic ecclesiology and the

---

[15]Murray, *We Hold These Truths*, pp. 27-142.

demands of our pastoral ministry require that this letter speak both to Catholics in a specific way and to the wider political community regarding public policy.[16]

Following this logic the letters are written so that the full religious-moral-social policy argument is spelled out, but the case for policy specifics is also cast in a way which those outside the community of faith can find persuasive.

I have described the pastoral-political style of the U.S. Bishops as "democratic" for two reasons. The *process* by which the pastorals are drafted has a democratic component and the *product* has a democratic function. The process of the pastorals involves not only the hearing of witnesses noted above, but also the circulation of drafts for public commentary. Those who have followed this process know the significant impact such commentary has had. This should not be taken as an indication that the bishops are conducting an opinion poll. The core of these pastoral letters is a normative doctrine which is in place; the commentary relates much more to the persuasive quality with which the moral doctrine is conveyed, the quality of the empirical analysis in the letters and the wisdom of the policy recommendations.

The inclusion of this "democratic" component in a Catholic teaching document must be carefully described. The bishops themselves distinguish different levels of religious authority within the same pastoral. This allows them to protect the status of binding general moral principles, but also to make specific moral choices without expecting the entire community of the church to be bound by the concrete policy options proposed in the letters. The fact that the bishops endorse a given option ("No First Use" of nuclear weapons; job training programs, etc.) will give it visibility and a certain weight in the public debate, but the very specificity of the choice guarantees

[16] *The Challenge of Peace*, #19.

and invites debate within the church and the society. The democratic component of the process is a reflection of several characteristics of the *Pastoral Constitution*: the effort to respect empirical analysis, to abide by the laws and procedures of secular disciplines, the desire to elicit the voice of the laity on secular questions and the willingness of the church to continue the dialogue with the world begun at Vatican II.

The product of the pastorals is democratic in the sense that they are designed as a contribution to democratic debate within society. The specific purpose of the bishops is to create space for the moral factor in the wider political argument. The bishops believe, in the style of the *Pastoral Constitution*, that they have something to learn from the world and something to teach the world. Although the pastorals enter the specifics of policy debate often, the bishops do not show any indication that their policy choices finish the debate. The specific choices of the bishops are meant to call others into the moral argument. In this way the moral dimensions of the policy debate are given more visibility, more time and space by the press and policy makers and, hopefully, more weight in the determination of policy.

The role for the pastorals makes the bishops actors in the democratic process. Their initial arena of influence is their own community; but the style of the pastorals and the process used makes them available to other constituencies. This is the arena of public opinion. The church's role in a democracy is directly tied to the ambit of public opinion. The bishops can abide strictly by the church-state provisions outlined in this paper and still be a constant factor in the formulation of public opinion.

Public opinion does not dictate public policy. But it does set a framework—establishing limits, giving weight to key values or issues—within which policy choices are made. By shaping public opinion it is possible to influence the direction of policy without necessarily dictating policy choices. By focusing on the moral quality of the public opinion debate and by being willing to address the moral dimensions of specific policy choices the U.S. Bishops are seeking to follow the invitation of Paul VI (to be actors in the development of Catholic social teaching), of Vatican II (to dialogue in-depth with the world) and John Courtney Murray (to assume responsibility for the moral consensus of a democracy).

The Protocols of Patriotism: Separatist Spirit and American Civil Religion

Catherine L. Albanese
Wright State University

On the Fourth of July, in 1788, Philadelphia had a memorable day. As the bells pealed joyously from the city's Christ Church, ten ships sailed onto the horizon, each waving a white flag inscribed with the name of a state that had ratified the Federal Constitution. Meanwhile, on the city streets, groups of people were beginning to muster, forming the great procession that would march through the day. As the procession took shape, the leaders took their places: "twelve axe-men, dressed in white frocks, with black girdles round their waists, and ornamented caps." Behind them could be seen a company of dragoons and a man mounted on a horse, "bearing the staff and cap of liberty; under the cap, a silk flag with the words *'fourth of July*, 1776,' in large gold letters."[1]

The event was the Grand Federal Procession, and in the

---

[1]For a full account of the Grand Federal Procession, from which description and quotations come, see Francis Hopkinson, *Account of the Grand Federal Procession in Philadelphia, July 4, 1788, to Which Are Added Mr. Wilson's Oration, and a Letter on the Subject of the Procession* (Philadelphia: Carey, 1788), pp. 1-14.

studied symbolism of its march, eighty-eight divisions succeeded each other in a line perhaps a mile and a half in length. In it, representatives of seemingly every trade and service offered by the new republic linked themselves to acclaim the Constitution. Carpenters and saw-makers marched; and so did printers and bookbinders, sailmakers and ship joiners, cabinet and chair makers, traders and merchants, and on through a litany of labor. Borne along in the parade, too, rode huge floats—grand constructions of the Constitution as the "new roof" and of the "federal ship Union"—and smaller ones of "federal flour," a "federal printing press," and the like. Themes related to the Federal Constitution were elaborated at far greater length and in far more intricate detail than can be captured here. Neither color nor prop was spared; and the result was as striking a visual representation as any organizer could hope to achieve.

Sandwiched among the eighty-eight divisions in this city of brotherly love, a telling sight, even among the more extravagant displays, could be seen. There, marching together in one division, were "the clergy of the different christian denominations, with the rabbi of the Jews, walking arm in arm." One observer, the noted Philadelphia physician Benjamin Rush, wrote to a friend that "pains were taken to connect ministers of the most dissimilar religious principles together, thereby to show the influence of a free government in promoting Christian charity."[2]

Amidst the ecumenism and good feeling, the iconography of the parade was proclaiming what, from a religious point of view, could be called a second revolution. The celebrated harmony of Jew with Christian and Christian with Christian came because, as the structure of the parade told eloquently,

---

[2]Benjamin Rush to Elias Boudinot [?], Philadelphia, 9 July 1788, in *Letters of Benjamin Rush*, ed. L.H. Butterfield (Princeton: Princeton University Press, 1951), 1:474. The same letter, without notation of its author, was bound with the Hopkinson account.

all had been assimilated into something higher—into the new religion of the republic with its sacred text in the Constitution. The procession was a great ritual, a cultus that enacted in space and time a patriotic creed about the meaning of life and of death. For the Grand Federal Procession spoke of ultimate powers embodied in the new American state. And it visually prescribed the ethical code that should govern the lives of patriots in every calling. Whatever they did as individuals, Americans were bound together in the unity of the nation, said the parade. However compelling their vocations in themselves, they all stood at the service of the state, which—as the procession also told—commanded their loyalties more.

The new religion Americans professed by gesture and deed has been named, since 1967, *civil religion*. And to its existence and nature scholars have devoted a flood of commentary. Whether Christians and Jews—and others who would follow them—gained or lost by pledging allegiance to the new religion became a question that, in our own times, troubled many. And indeed, the very name of the religion to which Jew and Christian were subscribing brought more than its share of academic attention. In the end, though, the term that the sociologist Robert Bellah chose—the term *civil religion*—has become linguistic coin.

When Robert Bellah published his epochal article "Civil Religion in America" in the journal *Daedalus* in 1967,[3] he was reviving a term that had earlier been employed by Jean-Jacques Rousseau in the setting of the French Enlightenment. According to Rousseau in *The Social Contract*, "the religion of the man and that of the citizen" could be distinguished; and in his subsequent reflections Rousseau offered his version of the difference. For us today, his assessment of the religion of the citizen, or "civil religion," is worth quoting at length, for it

---

[3]Robert N. Bellah, "Civil Religion in American," *Daedalus* 96 (Winter 1967), pp. 1-21.

bears directly on the issues that challenge civil religion scholarship. The religion of the citizen, Rousseau wrote,

> "is good in that it unites the divine cult with love of the laws, and that, in making the homeland the object of its citizens' admiration, it teaches them that all service to the state is service to its tutelary god. It is a kind of theocracy in which there ought to be no pontiff other than the prince and no priests other than the magistrates. To die for one's country is then to become a martyr; to violate its laws is to be impious. To subject a guilty man to public execration is to deliver him to the wrath of the gods."[4]

In spite of this positive, if pragmatic, estimate, Rousseau had further observations on the religion of the citizen that were less complimentary. "On the other hand," he went on,

> "it is bad in that, being based on error and lies, it deceives men, makes them credulous and superstitious, and drowns the true cult of the divinity in an empty ceremony. It is also bad when, on becoming exclusive and tyrannical, it makes a people bloodthirsty and intolerant, so that men breathe only murder and massacre, and believe they are performing a holy action in killing anyone who does not accept its gods. This places such a people in a natural state of war with all others, which is quite harmful to its own security."[5]

In this context, Rousseau proceeded to contrast the "religion of the citizen" with "the religion of man or Christianity"; not the Christianity "of today, but that of the Gospel." This, he

[4]Jean-Jacques Rousseau, *On the Social Contract* (1762), bk. 4, chap. 8, in Jean-Jacques Rousseau, *On the Social Contract, Discourse on the Origin of Inequality, Discourse on Political Economy*, trans. and ed. Donald A. Cress (Indianapolis: Hackett Publishing, 1983), pp. 99-100.

[5]*Ibid.*, p. 100.

said, was the "holy, sublime, true religion" in which "men, in being the children of the same God, all acknowledge one another as brothers." But unfortunately, thought Rousseau, the religion of man, or Christianity, had "no particular relation to the body politic." It was "a completely spiritual religion," and the terms "Christian republic" were "mutually exclusive." Christianity, he argued, "preaches only servitude and dependence," and "true Christians" were "made to be slaves." "They know it and are hardly moved by this. This brief life has too little value in their eyes."[6]

Hence, instead of the religion of man to support government, Rousseau looked to "a purely civil profession of faith" as a state necessity. "The dogmas of the civil religion ought to be simple, few in number, precisely worded, without explanations or commentaries," he wrote. In what was essentially a statement of Enlightenment deism, he named its "positive dogmas": "the existence of a powerful, intelligent, beneficient divinity that foresees and provides; the life to come; the happiness of the just; the punishment of the wicked; the sanctity of the social contract and of the laws." There was, asserted Rousseau, only one "negative" dogma that was necessary: that of intolerance. Civil and theological intolerance were "inseparable," and it was "impossible" for theological intolerance "not to have some civil effect." What followed, for Rousseau, was a plea for tolerance. "Now that there no longer is and never again can be an exclusive national religion, tolerance should be shown to all those that tolerate others, so long as their dogmas contain nothing contrary to the duties of a citizen."[7]

The plea for tolerance, published fourteen years before the events of 1776, was—certainly without the intention of its author—the shape of American things to come. Rabbi and Christian clergy, as they walked arm in arm in the Grand

[6]*Ibid.*, pp. 100-101.
[7]*Ibid.*, pp. 102-103.

Federal Procession in Philadelphia in 1788, performed in physical space the metaphysical doctrine. And nearly two centuries later, as Robert Bellah surveyed the past and present in American life, he captured the language of Rousseau in the designation *civil religion* and, as well, the structure of non-sectarian tolerance that Rousseau had identified as essential. Perhaps even more than Rousseau, because Bellah was troubled about America in the Vietnam era he looked to the bonding that civil religion brought. He turned, with a believer's expectation, to its ability to unite Americans and to make of them a mammoth national community.

"There actually exists alongside of and rather clearly differentiated from the churches an elaborate and well-institutionalized civil religion in America," Bellah wrote. He discovered the civil religion in the references to God in presidential inaugural addresses and "almost invariably to be found in the pronouncements of American presidents on solemn occasions." Building on years of sociological study, Bellah went on to find the civil religion in an annual ritual calendar, with holidays ranging from the Fourth of July and Thanksgiving to Memorial Day and Veterans Day and with a public school system to inculcate observance. And he found civil religion, too, in a series of sacred places like Gettysburg and Arlington National Cemeteries. "The separation of church and state," argued Bellah, "has not denied the political realm a religious dimension."

> "Although matters of personal religious belief, worship, and association are considered to be strictly private affairs, there are, at the same time, certain common elements of religious orientation that the great majority of Americans share. These have played a crucial role in the development of American institutions and still provide a religious dimension for the whole fabric of American life, including the political sphere. This public religious dimension is expressed in a set

of beliefs, symbols, and rituals that I am calling the American civil religion."[8]

Despite the reference to the "whole fabric of American life," it became clear, as the Bellah essay unfolded, that civil religion was religious nationalism in expressed and institutionalized form. Bellah, in fact, had framed his inquiry by reference to three wars—the Revolution, the Civil War, and the Vietnamese War—as times of "trial" for the civil religion. But unlike Rousseau, who had paradoxically wedded the tolerance of civil religion to its penchant for making "a people bloodthirsty and intolerant" and for rendering the killing of nonbelievers a "holy action," Bellah saw the nation's wars as occasions for positive growth. He did, it is true, try to push beyond the historical moments to which he had pointed. "The American civil religion," he observed, "is not the worship of the American nation but an understanding of the American experience in the light of ultimate and universal reality."[9] But even as he pronounced that judgment, in a curious turn, Bellah drew on a second departure from Rousseau's version of civil religion.

Earlier in his article, Bellah had made it clear that unlike the deistic God who remained eternally aloof—a principle of order and law more than a loving person—the God of American civil religion was "actively interested and involved in history, with a special concern for America." The civil deity evoked the tradition of ancient Israel and its God because, as Bellah asserted, the American civil religion had embraced the biblical theme. So it was that Bellah could end his essay with an evocation of biblical history. "Behind the civil religion at every point lie Biblical archetypes: Exodus, Chosen People, Promised Land, New Jerusalem, Sacrificial Death and Rebirth," he

---

[8]Bellah, "Civil Religion in America," pp. 1, 2, 11, 3-4.

[9]*Ibid.*, p. 18.

affirmed. "Genuinely American and genuinely new," the civil religion was also genuinely old.[10]

If so, Bellah had concluded on an equivocal note. The civil faith that signaled "ultimate and universal reality" also turned on the experience of an early group of English settlers in New England. For the seventeenth-century Puritan fathers had bequeathed to later generations of Americans the language of a new Israel in the New World. And their metaphor mediated power. As a generation of scholars have shown, the Puritan conviction that the God of Israel had bound himself in a new covenant with them had a profound effect on later American ideology—and history.[11] Inhabitants of the City upon a Hill, with the eyes of all people on them,[12] Puritans—and, learning from them, many later Americans—hailed the example to the nations that they were chosen to be. They hailed, too, the mission with which their status as the elect of God had taxed them, and they pledged themselves to the accomplishment of divine ends.

When the Puritan strand in American thought met the Enlightenment rhetoric of "nature and of nature's god" articulated in the Declaration of Independence, the American Revolution became the hinge on which the later civil religion turned.[13] Out of the encounter, finally, emerged a secular version of the Puritan New Israel. The old example and

[10]*Ibid.*, pp. 7, 18.

[11]For useful introductions, see Conrad Cherry, ed., *God's New Israel: Religious Interpretations of American Destiny* (Englewood Cliffs, N.J., Prentice-Hall, 1971), and Bellah himself in Robert N. Bellah, *The Broken Covenant: American Civil Religion in Time of Trial* (New York: Seabury Press, 1975).

[12]These familiar phrases are taken from the lay-sermon "A Modell of Christian Charity" (1630) by John Winthrop on board the *Arbella*. See, Winthrop, "A Modell of Christian Charity," in Perry Miller and Thomas H. Johnson, eds., *The Puritans: A Sourcebook of Their Writings*, rev. ed. (New York: Harper & Row, Harper Torchbooks, 1963), 1:199.

[13]For an extended argument in this vein, see Catherine L. Albanese, *Sons of the Fathers: The Civil Religion of the American Revolution* (Philadelphia: Temple University Press, 1976).

mission, which existed at the behest of a transcendent God, became under the new order an example of republican democracy and a mission to spread it to other, not-so-fortunate peoples. The transcendence of God, in the nineteenth-century atmosphere of confidence, became the transcendence of Americans.

Bellah himself, essentially positive about American civil religion, admitted in his book *The Broken Covenant* that "many of the spokesmen of secular culture uttered versions of the doctrine of America as a chosen people that would make a theologian blush."[14] But a second major scholar who found himself part of the civil religion debate was less critical. Writing out of a somewhat different and, in part, earlier conceptualization than Bellah's, Sidney E. Mead celebrated "the religion of the Republic," a religion with a "definable theological structure" providing legitimation for the Declaration of Independence and for the religious pluralism of the nation. This religion, he said, and "not the Christianity exhibited in the form of any or all of the denominations" was the "religion of American culture."[15]

Like Bellah, Mead understood what he saw as a religion existing alongside the churches; and, like him as well, he was impressed by its integrity. But perhaps more than Bellah, Mead, though a historian, was interested in the ideal order of this religion and not in its material and ceremonial specifics. Evoking the philosopher Alfred North Whitehead, he wrote of "man ... the animal that can cherish aspirations, which is to be religious, to be committed to an ideal world beyond the present world and to the incarnation of that ideal world in actuality." For Mead, to be committed to the religion of the Republic, therefore, meant "not to be committed to this world

---

[14]Bellah, *Broken Covenant*, p. 57.

[15]Sidney E. Mead, "Religion of (or and) the Republic" (1973), in Mead, *The Nation with the Soul of a Church* (New York: Harper & Row, 1975), p. 121; Mead, *Nation with the Soul of a Church*, p. 5.

as it is, but to a world as yet above and beyond it to which this world ought to be conformed."[16]

From this perspective, nationalism was "not necessarily absolutistic or idolatrous" for Mead. In fact, the religion of the Republic was "essentially prophetic." "Its ideals and aspirations" stood "in constant judgment over the passing shenanigans of the people, reminding them of the standards by which their current practices and those of their nation are ever being judged and found wanting." Most of all, this religion had been embodied in Abraham Lincoln, "the most profound and representative theologian of the religion of the Republic."[17]

Identifying with the lofty tradition he described, Mead looked at the saga of sectarianism in the United States with something approaching disdain. "Sectarianism," he explained, "means that each sect wants its particular forms to be imposed as God's will on all people." Thus, the historical and particularistic manifestations of religion in sectarianism were "a greater threat than secularism or outright atheism."[18] It was, seemingly, a peculiar stance for a historian—someone for whom particularity, for all its problems, should have inspired allegiance. But Mead honed his essentially theological position in a series of essays that praised the universal and questioned the denominational in American life.

Rousseau's negative doctrine of intolerance had come home with a vengeance in the work of Sidney Mead. Although Mead gave no indication of having read the French philosopher, his nonsectarian, general religion was predicated on a deism at home in the Enlightenment world. Indeed, he specifically, and in some theological detail, identified the religion of

[16]See Mead's note comparing his views to those of Bellah, in Mead, *Nation with the Soul of a Church*, pp. 129-130, n. 3; for the quotations, see Sidney E. Mead, (1967), *ibid.*, pp. 64-65.

[17]Mead, *ibid.*, pp. 64-65, 68.

[18]*Ibid.*, pp. 74, 76.

the Republic with the religion of the Enlightenment.[19] But the ceremonial protocols of Rousseau's civil religion were surely missing from the Mead account. And the ideological other side of Rousseau's civil religion—its potential for totalitarianism and bloodthirstiness—paled before the high rhetoric of Mead's transcendentalism. Mead did find the occasion to warn that "the primary religious concern in our nation must be to guard against national idolatry; against the state becoming God."[20] He certainly did not make that concern the primary one of his essays.

A third major scholar whose work was subsumed under the rubric of civil religion, however, did write passionately against idolatry. Well before Robert Bellah's model of civil religion had captured scholarly imaginations, Will Herberg had spoken of the American Way of Life.[21] And it was clear from what he described that he understood the American Way of Life in proportions that were larger than Bellah's later civil religion. Indeed, the American Way of Life was a greater circle that included the smaller circle of the Bellah model. For Herberg, the American Way of Life meant more than a set of sacred beliefs and behaviors related to the American government. And it found expression not only alongside the churches but also within and through them.

What Herberg had identified was American cultural religion (he did, in fact, call it "culture-religion"). From the first he made it evident that he viewed this religion as including "such seemingly incongruous elements as sanitary plumbing and freedom of opportunity, Coca-Cola and an intense faith in

---

[19]Mead, "Religion of (or and) the Republic," in Mead, *Nation with the Soul of a Church,* pp. 118-122.

[20]Mead, *Ibid.,* p. 76.

[21]See Will Herberg, *Protestant-Catholic-Jew: An Essay in American Religious Sociology,* rev. ed. (Garden City, N.Y., Doubleday, Anchor Books, 1960). *Protestant-Catholic-Jew* first appeared in 1955. Here and in what follows, I use the more readily accessible revised paper edition.

education—all felt as moral questions relating to the proper way of life." Later, writing after 1967 in the midst of the civil religion debate, Herberg insisted that American civil religion "though not generally recognized as such" was "fully operative in the familiar way, with its creed, cult, code, and community, like every other religion." In it, he thought, "religion and national life" were "so completely identified that it is impossible to distinguish the one from the other."[22]

In his earlier and now-classic *Protestant-Catholic-Jew*, Herberg had lamented a loss of ascendancy for the three traditional faiths, a condition in which "the faith itself [was] reduced to the status of an American culture-religion." What followed, for Herberg, was in some sense prophetic. He warned that Americanism, the "civic religion of the American people," could "serve as a spiritual reinforcement of national self-righteousness and a spiritual authentication of national self-will." "In its crudest form, this identification of religion with national purpose generates a kind of national messianism," admonished Herberg. And American religion was, for Herberg, pervasively idolatrous. "Not God, but man—man in his individual and corporate being—is the beginning and end of the spiritual system of much of present-day American religiosity," he wrote. By the seventies, the Jewish sociologist had not found reason to change his mind. He was still, in essence, a theologian, and his words were still those of pro-phetic condemnation. "To see America's civil religion as some-how standing above or beyond the biblical religions of Judaism and Christianity, and Islam too, as somehow including them and finding a place for them in its overarching unity, is idolatry, however innocently held and whatever may be the subjective intentions of the believers," Herberg concluded.[23]

[22]Herberg, *Protestant-Catholic-Jew*, p. 262, 75; Will Herberg, "America's Civil Religion: What It Is and Whence It Comes," in Russell E. Richey and Donald G. Jones, eds., *American Civil Religion* (New York: Harper & Row, 1974), pp. 76, 77.

[23]Herberg, *Protestant-Catholic-Jew*, pp. 262-264, 268; Herberg, "America's Civil Religion," p. 87.

Uninformed by Rousseau as he wrote, Herberg yet had more in common with the French philosopher than either Bellah, who had borrowed his language, or Mead, who had inherited his deism. Like Rousseau, he stressed the embodied nature of civil faith in behavior; and, like him as well, he understood it as potentially dangerous in its intolerance. But, parting company with Rousseau, Herberg could not advocate civil religion as a state necessity.

Bellah, Mead, and Herberg had all three ended differently. Measured against the civil religion of Jean-Jacques Rousseau, each had carved a position that bore some resemblance to the French philosopher's (without, except in the case of Bellah, indicating awareness). Yet each had carved a position that was distinctive and his own. Even so, for all their individual emphases, on the one hand, and their structural links to Rousseau, on the other, in one important respect the three were bound *together* and separated from the Frenchman. For each, a particular and distinctively American form of religious engagement generated thought. A specific and urgent moral theological question prompted each as he refined his understanding of the civil religion proposition. Was civil religion good and to be praised? So said Mead. Was civil religion idolatrous and to be condemned? So retorted Herberg. Was civil religion once good but now gone rancid and in need of deep revival? So, more and more, prophesied Robert Bellah.

In short, the civil religion debate was, as it still is, inexorably drawn into the patriotic myth—the sacred story of America— with which it deals. It became, and becomes so long as Americans struggle with it, scholarship within the myth.[24] Or, as John F. Wilson has observed with a bow to anthropology, it is "the ideological core of a revitalization movement." "The civil religion proposal, or the advocacy of a religion of the republic," Wilson wrote, "might be seen, finally, as the attempt, through

[24]For a fuller discussion, see Albanese, *Sons of the Fathers*, pp. 221-225.

a variety of particular forms, to distill the old political culture of the United States which was supported by a broadly Protestant establishment. The purpose is to conserve that culture even as it, and the associated establishment, is threatened from within and without."[25]

Working from the legacy of that civil religion proposal and the scholars who have generated the debate, it is difficult to pretend indifference—or to claim that somehow one has discovered the means to escape the interpretive circle. Indeed, this is why reflections on civil religion often seem so sterile, why nothing new seems to surface in the discussion of the "new" religion that, curiously, has become old and conservative. And this is why analysis continually seems to slide off into theological construction, into civil-religious building for the future. Yet, for all the snares, it is not altogether impossible, at least for a time, to separate description from prescription, to talk about what exists and to sift through some of its riddles. Perhaps one must be only half an American for the exercise: in any case, the trial at distance seems worth the effort. Rendering the familiar somehow incongruous—seeing it in a new way—can lead to a taste of the freedom that, we have been told, the liberal arts bring.

Surely, it is futile either to "propose" an American civil religion or to advocate its banishment. The evidence of the existence of one abounds around us, and the first generation of civil religion scholars have been joined by a cadre of others in marking its trail. As an exercise in following it anew, we have only to look at the recent explosion of the Challenger and the actions of Americans thereafter. Some reflection on

[25]John F. Wilson, *Public Religion in American Culture* (Philadelphia: Temple University Press, 1979), pp. 174-175. Wilson drew on the work of Anthony F.C. Wallace, for his concept of revitalization movements: See Wallace, "Revitalization Movements: Some Theoretical Considerations for Their Comparative Study," *American Anthropologist* 58 (1956), pp. 264-281.

the incident, however brief, will shed instructive light on the dynamics of the American civil religion.

The nation in miniature had gone up (in both senses) in the spacecraft: man and woman, Christian and Jew, white and black and even, with a touch of New Age plurality, Hawaiian of Japanese descent. The Challenger was Herman Melville's *Moby Dick* translated to a new medium and a new time. It evoked age-old archetypes of the hunt and its moral meaning, filtered through the Puritan lens of an errand into the wilderness.[26] Meanwhile, the new American ship, like Melville's *Pequod*, was a study in rigor and proper form and, at the same time, violent catastrophe. Tied to the history of the republic and to our own time, the Challenger encapsulated, in its familiar shuttle body, the American creed—loyalty to country and self-sacrifice for the national cause. And therein lay, too, its version of the American code. "To die for one's country," Rousseau had written, is "to become a martyr." This crew had implicitly said as much. The short-lived flight of the Challenger had been a hymn to the protocols of patriotism, and its litany, we discovered, was a litany of death, as the President—the high priest of the civil faith—led the nation in mourning.

Creed, code, cultus, and community—they unfold before us in concert in the Challenger's explosion. And the episode, in its complexity, reminds us of the series of contradictions that American civil religion involves. The millions who watched the spacecraft disintegrate were bonded without touching to a crew encased and then separated by the thrust of machinery

---

[26]For an account that reflects the values of the civil religion, see "A Nation Mourns," *Time*, 10 February 1986, pp. 20-35. Herman Melville's *Moby Dick: Or, The Whale* was first published in 1851. For reflections on the meaning of the hunt in *Moby Dick* in the context of American culture, see Richard Slotkin, *Regeneration through Violence: The Mythology of the American Frontier, 1600-1860* (Middletown, Conn: Wesleyan University Press, 1973), pp. 538-565. And for the "errand into the wilderness," see Perry Miller, *Errand into the Wilderness* (1956; reprint ed., New York: Harper & Row, Harper Torchbooks, 1964), esp. pp. 1-15.

from Canaveral below. The event suggested that the national government had acted in a quest for the ideal that, for all the reputed American materialism, never took matter seriously. Inside the craft, there were pluralities that reflected the nation's demographic composition, but there was no assurance that genuine pluralism—a pleased interior acceptance of the plural situation—flourished. Beyond that, in light of the plural ethos of the crew, the Puritan covenant and its attendant mission, which in secular guise had rendered trip and space program a moral imperative, achieved a special incongruity. And finally, at the lift-off of the ship, the startling juxtaposition of order and violence resonated, in its jarring rhythm, with an apocalyptic quality in American life.

It was truly a White Whale that the Challenger had chased, and the Whale was an ancient one that had trailed the *Arbella* and the *Mayflower* across the Atlantic in the seventeenth century. In a fact that we often forget, the Puritan impulse was a good example of what Sidney Mead has called sectarianism. The Puritans were, after all, a people who *withdrew*, who—whether they formally separated from the Church of England or not—shrunk from its corruption and impurities, banded together, and sailed across an ocean to inaugurate a pure and perfect commonwealth. Such is hardly a population from which promiscuous mingling and blending might arise. Moreover, the spiritual stance of separation in Puritan culture had been replicated physically in the geographical separation of the New World. The concern for purity, logically and psychologically, blurred into fear of pollution and contamination. A chosen people needed to be careful to preserve its specialness: it could not merge unthinkingly with the great unwashed.[27]

Because, as Robert Bellah tells us, the old Puritan covenant with Jehovah became the election of a proud and divinely

----

[27]The background for my analysis of purity and pollution here and later in the essay is the work of Mary Douglas. See Mary Douglas, *Purity and Danger: An Analysis of Concepts of Pollution and Taboo* (London: Routledge & Kegan Paul, 1966).

destined nation,[28] American civil religion protects the Puritan privilege. In the words of Rousseau, it "unites the divine cult with love of the laws," and it "teaches ... that all service to the state is service to its tutelary god." Whether it is also "based on error and lies" and "drowns the true cult of the divinity in an empty ceremony," we still need to determine. For now we can follow the trajectory of Puritan separation as it disappears into general American culture; and the task is not so difficult as at first it might appear. With an early ascendancy in the media—in the formal language of state, school, and church, and especially in print—the Puritan world view became part of the inheritance of a dominant and public center in American life.[29]

Intellectually, the Puritan tradition fostered idealism. Idealism, of course, is a mental instinct at least as old as Plato, a belief that ideas (and ideals) are more important than material realities, or—to put the case in the popular parlance of our time—that it is "better to be dead than Red." Or, again, to stand back from the shock of the example, the idealism of American life does what all idealism does: it transcends. It goes beyond the present world of flesh and time, preferring the universalizing and ahistorical to the concrete and ambiguous muddles of history. Thus, it is ironic, indeed, that the idealism of Sidney Mead may have had its roots in the sectarian vision of the Puritans.

But Mead was not alone. The idealist instinct has taken flesh in spite of itself in a self-conscious philosophical tradition extending from Jonathan Edwards and Ralph Waldo Emerson to Josiah Royce and Aldous Huxley. It has also taken flesh, in popular culture, in religious movements like Christian Science

[28]See, especially, Bellah, *Broken Covenant*, pp. 36-60.

[29]For further discussion, see Catherine L. Albanese, "Dominant and Public Center: Reflections on the 'One' Religion of the United States," *The South Atlantic Quarterly* 81 (Winter 1982), pp. 14-29.

and New Thought.[30] However, throughout American history a more generalized idealism was abroad in the land. Not simply a religio-philosophic tradition, this idealism was a popular state or quality of mind in which ideal constructions colored the everyday world through the power of imagination. Particular ideas and values so dominated the interpretive process of making sense of things that, in the final analysis, very little of the thing "out there" and very much of the image within controlled perception. "Spirit," if you will, triumphed over matter, and myth told new American tales that were strongly toned readings—or misreadings—of present events.[31]

To give a few examples, at the time of colonial settlement the exuberant promotional literature in old England advertised colonial paradises that existed only as new American dreams. Negatively, colonial fears of Indian menace were often projections of an inverted ideal upon "savages" dwelling in a wilderness. Similarly, in the era of the Revolution the vision of future greatness for a nation yet unborn was surely an ideal construction, while belief in the demonic prowess of the British was its negative.[32] By the nineteenth century, a generalized

[30]For discussions of philosophical idealism germane to this essay, see Herbert W. Schneider, *A History of American Philosophy*, 2nd ed. (New York: Columbia University Press, 1963), pp. 3-11, 161-177, 223-274, 375-430. For popular metaphysical movements, see J. Stillson Judah, *The History and Philosophy of the Metaphysical Movements in America* (Philadelphia: Westminster Press, 1967).

[31]My language here echoes Harold Bloom's understanding of strong "misreadings" or "misprisions" of literary texts. See Harold Bloom, *Agon: Towards a Theory of Revisionism* (New York: Oxford University Press, 1982), esp. pp. 16-51.

[32]For examples of promotional literature, see Louis B. Wright, ed., *The Elizabethans' America: A Collection of Early Reports by Englishmen on the New World* (Cambridge: Harvard University Press, 1965); Bradley Chapin, ed., *Provincial America, 1600-1763* (New York: Macmillan, Free Press, 1966); and Russel B. Nye and Norman S. Grabo, eds., *American Thought and Writing*, vol. 1, *The Colonial Period* (Boston: Houghton Mifflin, Riverside Press, 1965). For negative projections on American Indians by early New Englanders, see Peter N. Carroll, *Puritanism and the Wilderness: The Intellectual Significance of the New England Frontier, 1629-1700* (New York: Columbia University Press, 1969), pp. 76-79, 123-124, 147-153, 167-176, passim; and Slotkin, *Regeneration through Violence*, esp. pp. 65-93. And for ideal constructions at the time of the Revolution, see Albanese, *Sons of the Fathers*, pp. 66-68, 110-111, 90-95, passim.

idealism prompted continuing affirmations of an abiding moral order—a structure of law and decency to which society ought to conform. Catalyzed by growing technological achievement, it was present, too, in the firm belief in the idea of progress that pervaded the culture. But idealism, as "manifest destiny," also colored rationales for Indian Removal and continental expansionism. It controlled southern theological defenses of slavery based on the fittest arrangements, blessed by God, for an inferior race.[33] Again, in our own country, this generalized idealism offered justification for war "to make the world safe for democracy" or to bring the sacred gifts of freedom and democratic institutions to a Vietnam or a Grenada.

In each case, binding historical situations were broken or escaped by spiritual constructions that made ideas primary. Grand American ideas were there at hand, descended from above to modify the bleak outlines of earthly existence. All justified action by means of the imagination, and all, intriguingly, issued in pragmatic gains for those who held to them.

Pragmatic gains, however, draw us from the ideal to the social world. And here it may be argued that, socially, Puritanism fostered separation and, in its most exclusive form, racism. Although, from the 1840s, immigrants flooded the country to provide the labor that growth demanded, scholars of immigration, Will Herberg among them, have questioned the familiar image of the "melting pot."[34] In the ethnic backlash of the seventies and eighties, rather, it has become clear that

[33]For manifest destiny, Indian Removal, and natural law, see Albert K. Weinberg, *Manifest Destiny: A Study of Nationalist Expansionism in American History* (1935; reprint ed., Chicago: Quadrangle Books, 1963), pp. 72-99, 190-216. For an example of southern theological defense of slavery based on the idea of black racial inferiority and natural subordination to whites, see James Warley Miles, *The Relation between the Races at the South* (Charleston, S.C., Evans & Cogswell, 1861). For a discussion of Miles' thought regarding black inferiority and, also, of the thought of Edgar Gardner Murphy early in the twentieth century, see Ralph E. Luker, "Liberal Theology and Social Conservatism: A Southern Tradition, 1840-1920," *Church History* 50 (June 1981), pp. 193-204.

[34]See, for example, Herberg, *Protestant-Catholic-Jew*, p. 21.

pluralities have remained plural. Meanwhile, the myth of the covenant, of America as God's New Israel, can have weak appeal for many in ethnic groups who, with their own separate histories and concerns, find little in it that they can appropriate.

Yet there have been starker epiphanies to disclose the social underside of idealism. "Be not afraid of my body," the poet Walt Whitman had pleaded in the nineteenth century.[35] But, manifestly, Americans *were* afraid of bodies. The cult of sanitation that Will Herberg had noticed was only one sign. Enforced segregation and anti-miscegenation laws are others. Because, within the context of American society, miscegenation is a kind of ultimate example—the sexual acme of pollution fears—attitudes toward miscegenation are telling indicators. They suggest an elemental fear of contact at the center of the body politic, a mentality and habitual response that undercut the quest for community and mask a basic terror behind the protocols of patriotism.

Although sexual union between blacks and whites had been a fact of life in the English colonies—and in a place like Charleston, South Carolina, was even flaunted—from at least the 1660s the Virginia and Maryland legislatures had condemned the practice. "By the turn of the century," wrote Winthrop D. Jordan, "it was clear in many continental colonies that the English settlers felt genuine revulsion for interracial union, at least in principle."[36] Laws appeared on colonial books, and the laws of nature, too, were deemed to stand against such unions. In what was an unconscious, if twisted, tribute to the power of black blood, mulattoes (persons, here, with *any* admixture of African or Afro-American ancestry)

[35]The lines are from Walt Whitman, *Leaves of Grass* (1891-1892), in "As Adam Early in the Morning" (11.5) from "Children of Adam." See Whitman, *Leaves of Grass: Comprehensive Reader's Edition*, eds. Harold W. Blodgett and Sculley Bradley (1965; reprint ed., New York: W.W. Norton, 1968), p. 111.

[36]Winthrop D. Jordan, *White over Black: American Attitudes toward the Negro, 1550-1812* (Baltimore: Penguin Books, 1969), p. 139.

were designated "Negroes." A person was black who looked black, and even one great-grandmother could taint the purity of Caucasian blood.[37]

This colonial heritage of anti-miscegenation, without serious contest from the language or ideology of the Enlightenment, carried through the era of the Revolution. And if there had ever earlier been any question,[38] by the nineteenth century it was eminently certain that the true and genuine American, like James Fenimore Cooper's *Leatherstocking*, was racially unmixed, a "man without a cross" (of blood). White union with Indians seemed as repugnant as union with blacks; and, as Mabel Dunham insisted in *The Pathfinder*, "it would be a lighter evil to be killed than to become the wife of an Indian."[39]

After the beginning of the twentieth century, the unhappy career that awaited the offspring of a mixed racial union was still too evident, as the autobiography of Ely Green of Sewanee, Tennessee, illlustrates. The illegitimate child of a black woman and a white man from a prominent family of Sewanee, Ely—as he left the sheltering protection of childhood—

[37]The information on which this reading is based may be found in Jordan, *White over Black*, pp. 78-80, 136-178. For white-black sexual relationships in Charleston and the South Carolina-Georgia lowcountry in general, see also, Ira Berlin, "Time, Space, and the Evolution of Afro-American Society in British Mainland North America," *The American Historical Review* 85 (February 1980), p. 64.

[38]Jordan portrays colonial attitudes toward sexual union between whites and Indians as less severe than attitudes toward such union between whites and blacks (see Jordan, *White over Black*, pp. 162-163). For a general argument regarding the unimportance of racial conceptions in shaping early English colonial views of Indians, see Karen Ordahl Kupperman, *Settling with the Indians: The Meeting of English and Indian Cultures in America, 1580-1640* (Totowa, N.J.: Rowman and Littlefield, 1980).

[39]Leatherstocking calls himself a "man without a cross" in James Fenimore Cooper's *Leatherstocking Tales*. See, for example, James Fenimore Cooper, *The Last of the Mohicans* (1826; paper ed., New York: Airmont Books, Classics Series, 1962), pp. 66; and see the discussion in Slotkin, *Regeneration through Violence* (in a chapter significantly titled "Man without a Cross: The Leatherstocking Myth [1823-1841]"), pp. 493-494, 504-506, passim. For Mabel Dunham's remark, see James Fenimore Cooper, *The Pathfinder* (1840; paper ed., New York: Airmont Books, Classics Series, 1964), p. 100.

inhabited a demi-world in which he found community among neither whites nor blacks. He was, indeed, a "man with a cross," and the burden deeply disfigured and embittered him.[40]

Moments of epiphany such as these no doubt belabor the obvious. And, of course, there are distinctions to be made in a more systematic treatment of the material. But after the caveats and provisos are registered, there was a curious and destructive fastidiousness at the center of the New World adventure. Americans, following the Puritan lead, embraced the idea of new being without embracing its flesh.[41] Their newness was a creation of language—a transcendental reality that slipped past the occasions for genuine newness in their midst. In short, they wanted brotherhood and community—the lofty goal of their struggles to create a nation—but they did not want, to use the Mexican term, *carnalismo*.[42]

Caught in their idealism and mutual fear, with their symbols of purity and sanitation, Americans rejected the cultural and corporate unity that came with the mingling of flesh as well as spirit. Like so many isolated atoms, they were able to create a society that was mostly public and perfunctory, the functional society of political, economic, and cultural exchanges that enabled them to remain largely old and intact and, more and

[40]See Ely Green, *Ely: Too Black, Too White*, ed. Elizabeth N. Chitty and Arthur Ben Chitty (Amherst: University of Massachusetts Press, 1970), or—in the short version containing the account of Green's years at Sewanee—Ely Green, *Ely: An Autobiography* (New York: Seabury Press, 1966). For a general account of mulattoes and the Afro-American community in the United States, see Joel Williamson, *New People: Miscegenation and Mulattoes in the United States* (New York: Free Press, 1980).

[41]British colonial policy deliberately eschewed miscegenation. But in practice British theory could be swayed by existing conditions, as Winthrop Jordan's discussion of miscegenation in West Indian Jamaica makes clear. See Jordan, *White over Black*, pp. 140-143, 174-177.

[42]For *carnalismo*, see E.C. Orozco, *Republican Protestantism in Aztlán: The Encounter between Mexicanism and Anglo-Saxon Secular Humanism in the United States Southwest* (Glendale, Calif., Petereins Press, 1980), pp. 111, 148, 217, 223, passim.

more, privatized. By pushing community into the future as a far and nearly unattainable goal, they avoided the beginnings of community in the real men and women who were physically proximate.[43] Pollution had been contained and sanitation secured.

Such an analysis may seem to move from the premises of Herberg to the conclusions of Bellah. For Bellah has strongly argued his conviction that a disregard for the social whole through individualism and cultural particularism is destroying American society. And he has urged the restoration of community-through, however, a return to the covenantal myth of the Puritans in the civil religion.[44] But if Puritanism left a problematic intellectual and social legacy, we also need to ask, what did Puritanism foster politically? It is surely well to admire the roots of republican government in the Puritan covenantal bond. But looking at Puritan separatism for its political ramifications yields a different picture. We know that as they settled into New World life the Puritans became confirmed millennialists.[45] True to a sectarian pattern, they expected the second coming of Christ as an imminent event. They had read the Book of Revelation and knew well the

[43]My understanding here is informed by the thought of Wilson Carey McWilliams in *The Idea of Fraternity in America* (Berkeley: University of California Press, 1974), See, especially, pp. 1-8, 95-111, 618-624.

[44]For a useful statement of the problems of individualism and cultural particularism, see Robert N. Bellah, "Cultural Pluralism and Religious Particularism," in Henry B. Clark II ed., *Freedom of Religion in America: Historical Roots, Philosophical Concepts, and Contemporary Problems* (Los Angeles: Center for Study of the American Experience, The Annenberg School of Communications, University of Southern California, 1982), pp. 33-48. And for a classic statement of Bellah's call for a return to the covenant, see *Broken Covenant*, pp. 151-163.

[45]See, for example, Perry Miller, *The New England Mind: From Colony to Province* (1953; reprint ed., Boston: Beacon Press, 1961), pp. 185-190; and, for the eighteenth century, James West Davidson, *The Logic of Millennial Thought: Eighteenth-Century New England* (New Haven: Yale University Press, 1977). For a discussion of sectarian millennialism related to my understanding in this essay, see Catherine L. Albanese, *America: Religions and Religion* (Belmont, Calif., Wadsworth Publishing, 1981), pp. 137-140.

cataclysmic signs of his appearance; and, indeed, as they underwent Indian wars and sieges of domestic violence as well as pestilence and the like, they found the evidence for the approaching final day.

Placed beside the formal structure of the covenant, the millennial expectation acquires new meaning. The millennial day is an explosion *out* of protocol, a time of dramatic intensity in which the separation of formal contact is overcome in the *communitas* of eschatological violence. Political atoms, which normally do not touch, in the millennial moment can achieve the intense embrace of collision. Control can burst its bonds to run out of control: order can dissolve into disorder. Put another way, the instinct for intimacy—even intimacy in bodies politic—can impel a savage eucharist.[46]

What this suggests is a pattern—a grid—along which later American political life could be structured. The Puritan impulse-its firm, taut protocols punctuated by regular discharges of violence as a way, unconsciously, to end separation—became the American political way. Robert Bellah's evocation of three wars as times of trial in American life was poetically just. Historically, American isolationism has alternated with violent involvement in a kind of international bust and boom. In today's world, global repugnance at American pretensions and fear of its nuclear irresponsibility are, from one perspective, the inheritance of the millennial myth. Violence is, after all, a form of human contact.

The words of Rousseau return to haunt. The religion of the citizen was bad, he said, when "men breathe only murder and massacre," when they "believe they are performing a holy action in killing anyone who does not accept its gods." And the deposit of violence explodes in the American depositor's

---

[46]For *communitas*, see Victor W. Turner, *The Ritual Process: Structure and Anti-Structure* (Chicago: Aldine Publishing, 1969), esp. pp. 94-97. And for the language of the "savage eucharist," I am indebted to Slotkin, *Regeneration through Violence*, pp. 48, 124-125, 518-520, passim.

backyard. "This places such a people in a natural state of war with all others, *which is quite harmful to its own security.*"[47] Rousseau's somber comment takes us considerably further than the explosion of the Challenger, with which this reflection began. But the flight of the Challenger was, after all, not simply the innocent wide-eyed quest for knowledge that we sometimes associate with Canaveral efforts. Its enormous funding, its pressures for success, its wide publicity—with the Star Wars program ever on the horizon—suggest much more. It was a White Whale, indeed, that the Challenger pursued. And its voyage had begun with the Puritans.

From this perspective, the legacy of the American civil religion is surely an ambiguous one. Formal protocols interjected with bursts of violent patriotic spirit are not the cement with which to form cohesive community. Americans may well speak to their condition the words of Henry David Thoreau, framed in another situation but here nonetheless fitting.

> "I stand in awe of my body, this matter to which I am bound has become so strange to me. I fear not spirits, ghosts, of which I am one,—*that* my body might,—but I fear bodies, I tremble to meet them.... *Contact! Contact! Who* are we? *where* are we?"[48]

Civil religion has tried to provide answers to Thoreau's final questions. But, as John Wilson rightly noted, its answers are old and conservative. It is surely ironic that in the New World Americans have managed, in significant ways, to avoid the new.

[47]Emphasis mine.

[48]For Thoreau's words, written to describe his inner experience after climbing Mount Ktaadn in Maine, see Henry David Thoreau, *The Maine Woods*, ed. Joseph J. Moldenhauer, *The Writings of Henry D. Thoreau* (Princeton: Princeton University Press, 1972), p. 71.

Religion in America's Future: The Future of Religion in America

Denise Lardner Carmody

I propose to develop my theme in three unequal parts. First, I shall reflect on past experiments with religion in America;[1] second, I shall ponder the present configuration of American religion, using some of the work of Robert N. Bellah and his associates at the University of California, Berkeley;[2] third, I shall deal somewhat more fully with the future prospects and imperatives of American religion, paying special attention to the role I see for American Catholicism, the tradition from which I myself come. So, we have a survey in three parts, the first two of which ideally will recall ideas contemplated in earlier essays in this book, and the last of which will help us clarify our future agenda.

1. Historical Perspectives on American Religion

The separation of religious and secular zones that we present-

[1] See Jay P. Dolan, *The American Catholic Experience*, Garden City, N.Y., Doubleday, 1985.

[2] See Robert N. Bellah et al., *Habits of the Heart: Individualism and Commitment in American Life*, Berkeley: University of California Press, 1985.

day Americans experience is an historical anomaly.[3] Prehistoric peoples, as far as we can tell from their artifacts, lived in a highly sacral world, and creative scholars such as Mircea Eliade have greatly enriched our appreciation of how religious the life of hunting, the life of gathering, the life of early agriculture, and the life of early civilizations such as Sumer may well have been.[4] In Eric Voegelin's terminology, earliest humanity apparently lived within "the cosmological myth."[5] By this phrase Voegelin means the assumption or unquestioned conviction that the cosmos, the entire ordered world, composed a unity. Sky and earth, rock and plant, lizard and mammoth all were more like human beings than unlike us. Consequently, any fellow creature might occasion or convey a theophany: a manifestation of the power and holiness of the ultimately mysterious stuff that grounded the cosmic whole.

Recently I was reading Marguerite Yourcenar's wonderful historical novel, *Memoirs of Hadrian*. Although the emperor who is the main character ruled after the rise of Judaism and Christianity, his religious sensibilities continued to be those of the pagan Hellenistic world. Indeed, Yourcenar has done us the great favor of reminding us how urbane and refined such "paganism" could be, and thus why it was that many Romans and Greeks long despised Christianity as uncouth or narrowly sectarian. In her fictitious ruler's own words, Christianity, despite its appeal for the downtrodden classes, harbored considerable dangers: "Such glorification of virtues befitting children and slaves was made at the expense of more virile and more intellectual qualities; under that narrow, vapid innocence I could detect the fierce intransigence of the sectarian in the

---

[3]See Catherine L. Albanese, *America: Religion and Religions*, Belmont, Calif.: Wadsworth, 1981.

[4]See Mircea Eliade, *A History of Religious Ideas*, vol. 1, *From the Stone Age to the Eleusinian Mysteries*, Chicago: University of Chicago Press, 1978.

[5]See Eric Voegelin, *Order and History*, vol. 1, *Israel and Revelation*, Baton Rouge: Louisiana State University Press, 1956.

presence of forms of life and of thought which are not his own, the insolent pride which makes him value himself above other men, and his voluntarily circumscribed vision."[6] We may rightly feel that this judgment does Jesus of Nazareth a great injustice, but I think we can't honestly deny that the history of Christian persecutions too often has verified it.

At the moment, my main point is the cosmopolitan and cosmological religion of Hadrian and imperial Rome, which can stand duty for the great early civilizations generally. Hadrian thought of Roman religion as the mortar of his culture, but his thought was quite catholic or ecumenical. He was initiated in the Greek mysteries and studied Egyptian mortuary rites. He read the cynic philosophers and contemplated the caprices of nature and barbarities of social life that render the notion of a benevolent deity suspect. But he never doubted the potential sacrality of the occupation in which he was immersed at any time, whether it was war or administration, sexual pleasure or studying the stars. In his day, the cosmological myth still held.

So did the cosmological myth hold in the days of Confucius and Lao Tzu, along with the Chinese emperors who for centuries swam in their wake. So did it hold for most of the Indian emperors, Hindu or Buddhist, even after the thoughts of the Upanishads and Gautama that challenged it. The general story of humankind, for the majority of people right down to the past century, knew no violent disjunction between the sacred and the pragmatic. Further differentiations there of course were, especially in the West, as theology, philosophy, science, and political theory gradually became specialized occupations. But only very recently, and only in limited parts of the globe, did the distinction between the secular week and the vestigially sacral weekend that we now enjoy (or suffer)

[6]Marguerite Yourcenar, *Memoirs of Hadrian*, New York: Farrar, Straus & Giroux, 1984 (paper), p. 221.

come to obtain. Most other times and places thought differently. We will not get American religion into proper perspective until we appreciate what historian Sidney Mead called
"the lively experiment" that broke with this prior pattern. In
Mead's view, the establishment of the American venture in
pluralism, tolerance, and the separation of church and state
was as monumental as the establishment of Christianity in the
fourth century as the favored religion in the empire of Rome.[7]

From the titles of their essays, it appears that none of my
predecessors in this series paid great attention to the development of Christianity through the conciliar, medieval, and
reformation eras when the sense of church and state, of the
sacred and the secular, that Americans saw fit to try to change
developed. I shall only point out in passing that one of the
great problems American Catholics have had has been the gap
between the religious pluralism they experienced in this country
and the uniformity often expected by their religious leaders in
Rome. Only at the Second Vatican Council did the Roman
model of an established Catholic religion, with attendantly
lesser rights for other religious traditions, finally fall from its
pedestal. Americans could cheer that it was the brainpower of
John Courtney Murray and his like who pushed that idol
over, but the more historically minded among them, including
Murray himself, found a lot of scars to count.

The immigrant Christianity that Jay Dolan has described
draws much of its pathos from this context that I have been
trying to sketch. The majority of the Old World cultures from
which immigrant Christians came, perhaps especially in the
waves of the nineteenth century that brought the majority of
Roman Catholics and Eastern Orthodox, retained an ideal,
and usually a village life, that integrated religious faith with
daily work and local politics. This sort of unified culture holds
powerful attractions, as such diverse present-day examples as

[7]See Sidney Mead, *The Lively Experiment*, New York: Harper & Row, 1976.

the Polish popular resistance to Communism and the revivals of fundamentalist Islam should warn us. It punctuates the history of religion in America's past, if we do not avert our eyes from the terrible sufferings, cultural as much as physical, that Whites inflicted on American Indians. Blacks who came to this country as slaves from Africa fought valiantly to retain something of their African heritage, and so to keep the world from flying apart into chaos.

Thus, to be an immigrant more often than not has been to be a sufferer of violent assaults to one's sense of how God is in heaven and how all might be right with the world. Perhaps only the English colonists immigrated without having to submit themselves to a sundering greater entity, and certainly the psyches that they have passed down show that even their passage was very costly. When we look at the lively American experiment in pluralism we certainly find many things to praise, the ideal of mutual tolerance high among them. But we also find a break with the holism of premodern cultures that now presents us with some of our hardest questions. If we are not to try to answer such questions prematurely, by resorting to fundamentalist simplicities, we shall have to mature considerably beyond where most analysts of contemporary American religious culture now find us. This brings me to my second topic.

2. Present Configurations of American Religious Culture

It is no secret that fundamentalism now is a huge factor on the American cultural scene. If those who estimate the population of fundamentalists or evangelicals (I realize these two terms are not identical) at about 50 million are correct, one in five of our compatriots is trying to put Humpty-Dumpty back together again by making the nearly literal word of the Bible the basis for a new unification of the sacred and the secular. Those who would develop a critical intelligence, either academic or religious, find themselves running smack up against

these significant numbers. When the bruising has been especially bad, judgments of Hadrian about Christianity can seem all
too accurate. Like Augustine and Luther on their bad days,
we can come to feel that mass religion is a plague: pearls
before swine. The better tactic, then, probably is to recall that
200 million Americans may not be putting their brains into
zip-lock bags and so deserve our hopeful attention.

If we attend in the sociological spirit of Robert Bellah, or in
the philosophical spirit of Alasdair MacIntyre, however, we
shall still find miles to go before we sleep.[8] These two distinguished analysts agree that much of what disturbs them
about present American culture can be summarized under the
entry "therapy." In using their negative criticisms to try to
advance us another stage toward the future, I want to stress,
however, that "therapy" has an older and still valid set of
connotations, most of them thoroughly positive. The medical
doctor, nurse, physical therapist, speech therapist, psycho-
logical counselor, and the like who intervenes to heal people's
pains certainly is doing good work. Indeed, little is needed to
make such work religious: filled with the unconditional love
that Bernard Lonergan has made the hallmark of religious
conversion.[9]

What Bellah and MacIntyre criticize is the narcissism latent
in therapy, when it shifts from being a rare happening and
becomes a constant preoccupation. We can laugh at this
possibility as long as we think only in terms of weekly trips to
the dentist or the proctologist. The laugh starts to fade, however, when one visits California and meets the counseling
industry, so organized that it could follow you from cradle to
grave. And if one is willing to cast a critical eye at religious
literature, the visage can actually become grim. Have our

---

[8]See Alasdair MacIntyre, *After Virtue*, Notre Dame, Ind.: University of Notre
Dame Press, 1981.

[9]See Bernard J.F. Lonergan, *Method in Theology*, New York: Herder & Herder,
1972.

people indeed become so wounded that only the lacerated would presume to minister to them? Do the majority in fact feel so bad about themselves that it is foolish to repeat Jesus' command about love of neighbor? If sizable portions of our citizenry and churchgoers now do think of themselves as needing therapy, not in the old sense of regularly needing to confess their sins and receive the forgiveness and renewal of their God, but in a new sense of regularly needing to hear from counselors, be they professionals or peers, never-discouraging words, we have swapped our birthright for a mess of pottage.

Robert Bellah, thinking of the vigorous early American culture that Alexis de Tocqueville observed in the 1830s, rightly worries that narcissism is eroding our public-spiritedness. Alasdair MacIntyre, thinking of the Aristotelian tradition of the virtues, worries that modern culture has left us uncritical and normless. I myself, being a simpler religious type, wonder that so much talk takes so long to realize the priority of silence. Two-thirds of our personal and civic problems, I am convinced, stem from our ignorance of contemplation and our lack of religious asceticism. If we had the sense to learn from Job and rise early enough to catch the morning stars singing together, our days would be considerably less disordered.

This is rather negative, even carping observation, however, so I'd best move on from it. Bellah and his fellow researchers certainly found across the breadth of this land many people who do gain the wisdom of religious simplicity and who do pay themselves out, day by day, for the sake of their families and their towns. Alasdair MacIntyre certainly found a great many changes since the day of Aristotle, many of them of such a nature as to call the classical conception of the virtues into serious question. As the American Catholic Bishops, among others, recently have reminded us with reference both to the buildup of nuclear arms and to the functioning of our economy, great patches of our culture now run as it were independently of human control. Those of you who rush to the post office to mail your tax returns certainly know what I mean. In fairer perspective, then, we certainly have to give our contemporaries credit for coping with systemic forces that prior generations, including even very recent ones, never experienced. When what one finds at work doesn't make sense, and what one reads in the newspapers seems a script from an asylum, and every newscast within hearing is warning of fraud or drugs, the uterine circle of therapeutic kindness can seem necessary as well as comforting. As those who advertise so cleverly for scotch and perfume, for Wall Street investing and German imported cars, tellingly try to persuade us: We've earned it.

What, though, about the people who have spurned it? What about those who still think that developing an expertise that furthers knowledge or serves the common good is the prime test of education? What about those who still think that Christian churches exist to proclaim the good news of Jesus Christ, a criminal whom his followers found to have words of eternal life? They—let us hope we may say "we"—often don't fit the profile of therapeutic America, or of secular America, or of economic America, or even of fundamentalist America. Are they—we—right to think that they are continuing the more central traditions of American religion? Is there merit in their claim that love of God and love of neighbor still comprise the best program for American or world prosperity?

I shall take up these questions momentarily, when we turn to the matter of the future of American religion. Then I shall not disguise my conviction that a radically Christian contemplation and political action comprise the major portion of what our country needs if it is to have a blessed religious future. Here let me fill out the sketch of present American religion by referring to the many works of Robert Coles, the child psychiatrist who has studied "ordinary people" South and North, West and East. One of Coles' main tenets is that ordinary people are right to distrust the categorizations of academic types, since such categorizations nearly always fail to render the complexity and diversity of any individual life.

With poor children, mountaineers, Eskimos, rich children, Chicanos, maids, chauffeurs, and all sorts of other people, Coles has shown himself very sensitive to what a theologian like me tends to call "prevenient grace." Long before he or any other articulate, verbal type came into these people's situations to help name the wonders and the tragedies, the Spirit of God was at work washing what was dirtied, watering what had become parched, urging people easily rendered hopeless not to give up but to find reasons, usually other people, for whom to go on.[10]

In the ultimate perspective that theology and the millennial history of religious humanity offer, most of our contemporaries, like most of their forebears through time, have shown remarkable grace through lives of remarkable challenge if not outright suffering. Despite all my caveats about the narcissism of today's American culture, I continue to believe that God has not left herself without witness anywhere. Everywhere, God no more abandons people than a nursing mother abandons her child.

3. The Future Prospects and Imperatives of American Religion

What, then, seems to lie ahead for the American earth, if it would be fair, or for the American people, if we would be wise? Judgments obviously vary greatly in this matter, but you have invited me to deploy my crystal ball, so it is my own intuition that I shall be exercising from here on in to the finale. I had my intuition sharpened of late by a poll published in *The National Catholic Reporter*, so I shall begin by agreeing and disagreeing with what some other supposed experts have opined.

[10]See, for example, Robert Coles, *Children of Crisis*, vol. 5, *Privileged Ones*, Boston: Atlantic/Little-Brown, 1977, and Robert Coles and Jane Coles, *Women of Crisis*, New York: Delta/Seymour Lawrence, 1978.

The poll of the NCR that I have in mind took place prior to the recent Synod of Catholic Bishops in Rome. Various people, supposedly well-placed, were asked to list the items they thought ought to top the agenda of the Synod. The assumption was that this constructed agenda might represent wisdom about the most pressing problems facing our world and church in the years ahead. To my comfort and challenge, such familiar matters as nuclear disarmament, economic justice, and overcoming sexism ranked high on the experts' list.

The people, drawn from all over the country, obviously realized that nuclear weapons imperil all peace, domestic and foreign, psychic and social. They realized, as well, that military and diplomatic shuffles will mean nothing, unless the economic systems of our world are converted to the biblical reality that no people are blessed until justice rolls down like a mighty stream for all people. And the experts polled by the *National Catholic Reporter* also showed themselves well aware that the pervasive double-standard by which women remain second-class citizens is one of the most glaring patches of sin on the globe—all the more so when it can seem to claim fair housing in the Christian church.

These three perceptions, along with several lesser ones, encouraged me to think that many religious Americans do now appreciate the proportions of the tasks that lie ahead, if the traditions of either our nation or our predominant religions are seriously to engage the evils which mottle life for billions of our fellow human beings. Nonetheless, I was also struck by two omissions. The list of most pressing problems failed to include either ecological dangers or increased understanding among the world religions. So, as my first flyer into the American religious future that I hope will develop, let me briefly reflect on these two matters.

You are no doubt well aware that ecological problems have not atrophied merely because OPEC can't get its seven heads together and breathe a concerted fire. I live in a state being devastated by the drop in oil prices—Oklahoma probably will suffer a $500-million deficit in the state budget, most of which will mean fewer services for the most needy. But the deeper crisis facing Oklahoma and the rest of the planet is not economic but ecological: the pattern of erosion, depletion, and pollution that each year worsens the taint to such crucial systems as water, land, and air. The brute fact is that our current, industrialized way of life is incompatible with the planet we have inherited. Each time you read of chemicals spilled on the highway or feed poisoned by pesticide, you are being prodded by only the tiniest tip of the iceberg. The base of ecological pollution is an incredibly profound disorder.

A decade ago there was a well-marked debate about the responsibility for ecological pollution that we ought to lay at the door of biblical religion. The debate came to no clear-cut resolution, but any with ears to hear realized that biblical religion—Judaism, Christianity, and Islam—does harbor the significant danger of anthropocentrism: making human beings the pivot of creation and forgetting that God also called all the other species good. The better strands of biblical religion remind us that we are at most stewards of nature, and that no fellow creature should have to suffer our wanton abuse—because all of us creatures belong not to ourselves but to the God who made us from nothingness.

It seems to me that the omission of ecology from the agenda of what religious people ought to be concerned about in the next decade is not only a grievous failing in itself, but that it also suggests disturbing things about current American religion—things all too compatible with narcissism and excessive concern for therapy. Before turning to this consideration, however, let me attend briefly to the second topic whose omission from the agenda disturbed me: concern for the world religions. If this omission, too, turns out to imply an excessive self-concern, we may well find near to hand most of the religious remedy we need.

The case for the significance of nature and ecology can be boiled down into numbers: Creation has existed nearly 20 billion years; humankind only arrived on the scene in the last minutes of the cosmic day; the activity of God in caring for so many species other than us ought to tell us volumes about the divine transcendence: about how God is not anthropocentric, is not a God we can lug around in our back pocket. A similar case leaps forth from the figures about the world religions: Christians and Jews combined make up less than one-quarter of the world's population. If God does desire the salvation of all people, as the New Testament asserts (1 Tim 2:4), then the majority of divine concern and grace takes to different waters than those in which we swim.

I have tried to make this point, sweetly and gently, when involved in ecumenical discussions with different Christian groups. I have tried to make it when involved in ecumenical discussions between Christians and Jews. My distinct impression is that my fellow-discussants are about as interested in the world religions as Oklahoma oil men are interested in ecological apocalyptic. Even after I've tried to give both groups many benefits of the doubt, I have to say that I can't judge their attitude a positive sign of the Spirit of God. When I take what I feel them projecting into the arena of what Christians traditionally have called the discernment of spirit, most of the assessments turn out to be frighteningly negative.

What many analysts seem to see in such cases as the nuclear arms race, economic injustice, sexism, and racism is our need for deeper change. Often they use the language of conversion or reconversion, and I find that language congenial. What few religious analysts seem to see is the quite exact parallel in the case of the rights of nature and the rights of people who don't adhere to the Jewish or Christian traditions. There, too, we need deeper change. There, too, our present attitudes cry out for conversion. In bleak moments, I wonder whether it is realistic to expect even ten percent of our people to give up the materialistic assumptions on which our present industrial economy and militarism are based. Similarly, I wonder whether it is realistic to expect that even ten percent of Christians and Jews would adjure the profit they have drawn from the notion of "chosenness" or "election" and start to deal with other people as their exact equals in the love of God.

Such realism no doubt is a heavy burden to the sage, who has to be concerned about the prudence and likelihood of her counsels. The prophet has historically been granted more indulgence, it being considered sufficient for her to speak effectively to a remnant. Actually, I think of myself as working right now neither as a sage nor a prophet. Rather, I think of myself as trying to share with you the fragile seeds of a better future—the best intuitions I have of where the path of life may lie. When I reflect on the religious implications of the gross dysfunctions that presently spoil human life around our globe, it seems to me fairly clear that the twofold commandment in which Jesus summarized his message is as relevant as if he had spoken it yesterday.

Let me attempt to cast the best of the American religious tradition in the light of this twofold commandment. First, we are to love the Lord, our God, with all our minds, hearts, souls, and strengths. Doing this, we shall have little temptation to idolatry, chauvinism, or the abuse of nature. The Lord, our God, is the creative mystery that is nonpareil. At the beginning, the beyond, the depth, and the quiet center of every experience, our God lingers as the beauty, power, and love that makes us be. Though a thousand illusions fall at our right side and a thousand miseries clamor at our left, our mysterious, aboriginal God does not falter. Through sunrise and sunset, our God makes his light to shine on just and unjust alike, patiently hoping for our conversion. When we praise the American traditions of common sense and justice, we can reach back to this biblical foundation. As long as Israel, old or new, hears that the Lord, its God, is only one, it will know in its bones that the gross national product, the budget of the Department of the Defense, and the crazed Marxists supposedly marshaling on the border of Honduras are usually a distraction. If we loved the Lord, our God, so that all that was in us blessed his holy name, we would see that usually we flee to these idols because we don't want to do the justice God perhaps too gently asks of us.

The readout is much the same when we punch in Jesus' second commandment. According to the man who became the first-born from the dead, we are to love our neighbors as ourselves. The love that could carry us into the deathlessness of God knows little distinction between mine and thine, between male and female, between Gentile and Jew, between slave and free. The fathers of the church who judged that no one has the right to luxuries as long as anyone lacks necessities had appropriated the second commandment of Jesus. The theologians, such as Karl Rahner, who find a unity between love of God and love of neighbor have appropriated Jesus' in-given Spirit.[11] Radically contemplative and radically political, the love of God poured forth in our hearts by the Holy Spirit might convert us to the pathways, ecological and world-religious, economic and peace-making, that lay open a very fair future. As it was in the days of Deuteronomy, the choice is ours. God continues to set before us, this day, two ways, of life and of death. Therefore, shall we choose life?

If we wish to choose life, as religious citizens of the United States, we shall have to gird our loins for some encounters with death, the forces and forms of which are legion. We have alluded to the death symbolized by the cold, phallic missiles that seem to epitomize modern culture gone mad. We could conjure up the faces of the millions of the world's starving people, who would be happy in the first instance just to gain access to the wealth that the Northern nations waste. In the second instance, we would have to contemplate the perversions of the economic systems dedicated to keeping such millions in their desperate places. And then, unfortunately, there might

[11]See Karl Rahner, *Theological Investigations*, vol. 6, Baltimore: Helicon, 1969, pp. 231-249.

come to mind the leaders that we Americans lately have been supporting—such handsome specimens as Anastasio Somoza and Ferdinand Marcos, true beauties both.

A healthy American religious future, it seems to me quite clear, will depend on our expressing quite exactly the judgment we make of criminals such as Marcos and Somoza and then delivering to those who fostered them the political conse-quences. Is it too much to ask that our President be a person of intelligence and integrity, skilled and determined enough to ensure that people whom we support are minimally admirable? Or have we in fact chosen our pathway, saying that we aspire to nothing more than leading the world in materialistic af-fluence? I don't like to ponder politics, because the most obvious data, the candidates and the votes, are so discouraging. "My people, what have I done to you? In what have I offended you? Answer me!"

Politically, then, religious Americans of the last sixth of the twentieth century would be wise to batten their hatches. If they are not just nominal adherents of biblical religion, they must know that the ways of the twofold commandment of Jesus are as far from the ways of Washington and Moscow as the heavens are above the earth. Ecclesiologically, things some-times seem all too parallel. One would have thought that the example of Pope John XXIII would last at least twenty-five years, but apparently the Congregation for the Doctrine of the Faith doesn't think John XXIII had any theological signif-icance. Charity, freedom, creativity, the assumption of loyalty until disloyalty has been proven, and above all honesty—these apparently are of little account. John's motto, one recalls, was the ancient "In necessary things, unity; in dubious things, liberty; in all things, charity." Apparently masturbation, steril-ization, contraception, and other sexual concerns are thought matters of central moment, capable of determining whether one is moved by the Spirit of God, who of course continues to breathe where She will. What is one to do with religious authority, when it becomes so eccentric? Who will deliver us from the bondsmen of death?

In Margaret R. Miles' lovely work, *Image as Insight*,[12] we find art history set in the service of reordering the story of how the Christian rank and file of past eras thought about their God and themselves. The simple, unlettered people who depended on the sights they saw in the medieval churches learned that one could tell people by their characteristic features. Thus in the paintings of Giotto, one of Miles' favorites, Mary Magdalene regularly appears with long, flaming red hair, a great symbol of the ardent love that Jesus awakened in her by forgiving her sins. By what analogous features shall we pick out our genuine shepherds? The test that Jesus himself favored, we recall, was a matter of fruits. We could know what people, doctrines, proposed courses of action, and pathways into the future were most godly by the fruits, the religious life, they produced. To conclude this consideration of the future of American religion, let me specify the fruits or traits I think will prove most crucial.

First, there is the matter of honesty, a matter especially germane to all institutions of learning. Honesty need not mean imprudence, of course, but it cannot mean dissembling or keeping quiet, if either would distort what the Spirit of God presently seems to be saying. So all of us, clergy and laity, professors and students, have to express the faith that is in us. If those entrusted with the defense of *sacra fides* judge our faith inopportune, or untraditional, or dangerous, so much the worse. We shall have to trust that our institutions of learning value honesty and competence more than a party line. I noticed that in Karl Rahner's beautiful little book, *I Remember*,[13] there was little concern with what Roman authorities thought. If a former junior colleague such as Josef

[12]See Margaret R. Miles, *Image as Insight: Visual Understanding in Western Christianity and Secular Culture*, Boston: Beacon, 1985.

[13]See Karl Rahner, *I Remember: An Autobiographical Interview*, New York: Crossroad, 1985.

Ratzinger was put out by Rahner's defenses of Latin American theologians such as Gustavo Gutierrez, too bad. Rahner meant no offense, and he was slow to take offense. Mainly he just continued working, absorbed with the mystery of God, concerned to speak the truth which that mystery gave him to speak. It understates the case to say there is a lesson there.

Second, the lesson I find for our participation in American lesson civic life is much the same. Our job, I believe, is to go to the roots of our heritage and derive the most blazing love of neighbor and divinity we can. We ought then to propose, to commit ourselves to, the programs that such love tends to create. Others may disagree, but I think such programs will aim at producing intelligent political leaders, free-spirited church leaders, greater rights for marginalized people, the diminution of militarism, the full contribution of women, the defense of the unborn, intellectual honesty at every level, and friendly, irreverent, joyous love whenever possible. There is a time to mourn, of course, and frequently we will find ourselves in it. But we ought to find, more often, times to rejoice—times in the wake of Easter, when the seams of "possibility" cracked and, behold, God made all things new. This creativity is our best heritage. As American and religious people, we have received a sense of time and a sense of God in which all things can be made new. Let's make sure we use it to pressure the future to bring forth fruits worthy of the pain and the love that have made our country. Let's make sure the lively experiment continues to be worthy of our God.